ESSENTIAL
PSYCHOLOGY
General Editor
Peter Herriot

A9

FIRST EXPERIMENTS IN
PSYCHOLOGY

ESSENTIAL

PSYCHOLOGY

FIRST
EXPERIMENTS IN
PSYCHOLOGY

John M. Gardiner
and Zofia Kaminska

Methuen

First published in 1975 by Methuen & Co Ltd
11 New Fetter Lane, London EC4P 4EE
© 1975 John M. Gardiner and Zofia Kaminska
Printed in Great Britain by
Richard Clay (The Chaucer Press), Ltd
Bungay, Suffolk
ISBN (hardback) 0 416 81680 0
ISBN (paperback) 0 416 81690 8

We are grateful to Grant McIntyre of Open
Books Ltd for editorial assistance in the
preparation of this Series.

Contents

Preface

The aim of this book is to introduce the basic principles of experimental design in the context of carrying out experiments. None of the experiments requires previous knowledge of experimental psychology and very few require special laboratory equipment.

The statistical analyses used in this book are clearly explained in Steve Miller's *Experimental Design and Statistics* (A8 in *Essential Psychology*).

We have drawn on our experience, first as students, then as teachers, of courses in experimental work in psychology. We are indebted to those teachers who introduced us to experimental design, and to our students for contributing valuable feedback.

We would like to thank Steve Miller and Maggie Pool for their helpful comments, and Frances O'Sullivan for typing the manuscript so swiftly.

John M. Gardiner
Zofia Kaminska
1974

Editor's Introduction

Experiments are an essential part of psychology. We tend to pay a lot of attention to what we know about people, and to the concepts we use to try to describe and explain this knowledge. We often neglect *how* we acquire the knowledge we have. One method of acquiring such knowledge is by means of experiments. Some psychologists consider it the most worthwhile method, since it embodies the scientific elements of prediction and control; prediction of how people will perform at a given experimental task and control of as many irrelevant factors as possible so that the results can be explained in only one way. The books in Unit A of Essential Psychology deal mostly with facts and theories based on experimental evidence of this sort. John Gardiner's and Zofia Kaminska's book provides instructions on how to carry out some specific experiments. If read (and acted upon) in conjunction with Steve Miller's book *Experimental Design and Statistics* (A8), it should result in an appreciation of the difficulties and yet of the excitement of obtaining this sort of evidence.

What unifies Unit A of *Essential Psychology* is the notion of the human being as a processor of information. Like a computer we can register information, code it, perform operations on the coded version, store the result, and subsequently retrieve it. Moreover, like a computer, we can use our output, or behaviour, as feedback or evidence by which to monitor our subsequent performance. The authors in Unit A are more concerned with making generalizations about people than with

9

exploring their individual differences. Further, they deal with personal mental processes rather than with interpersonal social processes. They also probably place more stress on the traditional scientific experiments as a source of evidence than do most of the authors of the other units.

The computer analogy is very useful for handling the sort of evidence we get from experiments. For most experiments provide the experimental subject with input or information through the senses and then subsequently measure behaviour, or output; they then make inferences about the processes which occur between the two observable events. However, the computer analogy may not be suitable for handling other situations, where there is no immediate sensory experience or no easily identifiable consequent behaviour. And some psychologists also feel that it detracts from the concept of the individual as a person who can consciously act upon and control his environment. The reader will find other general conceptual frameworks in other units. Psychology is struggling to do justice to the complexities of its subject matter; it is hardly likely to find any single analogy to encompass the richness of human behaviour and experience. Coming to terms with a variety of explanatory frameworks decreases our confidence in psychology as a mature science; but perhaps it is best that we should be honest about what we don't know.

Essential Psychology as a whole is designed to reflect the changing structure and function of psychology. The authors are both academics and professionals, and their aim has been to introduce the most important concepts in their areas to beginning students. They have tried to do so clearly but have not attempted to conceal the fact that concepts that now appear central to their work may soon be peripheral. In other words, they have presented psychology as a developing set of views of man, not as a body of received truth. Readers are not intended to study the whole series in order to 'master the basics'. Rather, since different people may wish to use different theoretical frameworks for their own purposes, the series has been designed so that each title stands on its own. But it is possible that if the reader has read no psychology before, he will enjoy individual books more if he has read the introductions (A1, B1, etc.) to the units to which they belong. Readers of the units concerned with applications of psychology (E, F) may benefit from reading all the introductions.

A word about references in the text to the work of other

writers – e.g. 'Smith, 1974'. These occur where the author feels he must acknowledge by name an important concept or some crucial evidence. The book or article referred to will be listed in the references (which double as name index) at the back of the book. The reader is invited to consult these sources if he wishes to explore topics further.

We hope you enjoy psychology.

Peter Herriot

A Brief Glossary of Terms

Design The plan of the experiment, its logical structure.

Variable Literally, anything which is free to vary. An independent variable is one which is manipulated by the experimenter. A dependent variable is one which is measured by the experimenter. The aim is to see if changes in the independent variable lead to changes in the dependent variable.

Effect Changes in the dependent variable are often referred to as 'effects'. If the experiment is properly designed, one can attribute the cause of such effects to the changes in the independent variable.

Control Refers to the procedures one adopts, in designing an experiment, to try to ensure that any changes in the dependent variable are due solely to one's manipulation of the independent variable.

Condition Refers to a particular value, or level, of an independent variable.

Subject The experimenter's term for an individual who participates in his experiment. Often abbreviated to S.

Independent design One in which different subjects are assigned to each experimental condition. Also called a between-subjects design, or an unrelated design.

Related design One in which the same subjects serve under each experimental condition. Also called a within-subjects design.

Part One
Introduction

Our objectives

Our major objective is to introduce you to some of the basic principles and problems involved in designing and carrying out a psychology experiment. In the main part of the book we describe a number of experiments in sufficient detail for you to carry them out yourself, and in the final part of the book the aim is to encourage you to think up and design your own original experiments. In completing this book, we hope that you will acquire sufficient expertise not only to be able to design original experiments, but also to be able to criticize and evaluate other experiments you may read about – including those we present earlier in the book.

In addition to initiating you into the delights and mysteries of experimental design, our book is intended to 'service' the other texts in Unit A of the *Essential Psychology* series. These texts describe the results of particular experiments, or particular types of experiment, in the context of evaluating and describing the current state of knowledge in certain fields of psychological study. Our book should give you a fairly vivid impression of the work involved in carrying out and interpreting such experiments.

This is a 'working' book. While you could, of course, try reading straight through it, we do not recommend this approach. Our intention is that you work through the various experiments we describe. We assume, therefore, that you are strongly motivated to learn how to do experiments in psychology and that you are prepared to devote a certain amount of time to achieving that goal.

We assume also that your knowledge of experimental psychology is slight and in introducing each of the experiments we do not take any knowledge of the particular topic for granted. The other texts in Unit A will give a more detailed background to particular topics.

While we hope that the book may be useful to those of you beginning a degree course in psychology, we have assumed that many of our readers will be students on introductory courses in psychology which do not necessarily lead to specialization in psychology. For this reason, most of the experiments we describe do not require any specialized psychology apparatus. Indeed, many of our experiments can be carried out quite well at home, using 'apparatus' no more sophisticated than pencils and paper. Though the book could be used by an individual working alone, the ideal context for the book is an introductory psychology course.

Finally, we assume that you will also be prepared to buy Steve Miller's *Experimental Design and Statistics* (A8); this book was planned jointly with ours, and we do not give any help at all on statistical analysis except for suggesting what analyses are appropriate for each particular experiment. We assume that you will use Steve Miller's text in conjunction with our book and emphasize that, without his text, you will not be able to interpret the results you obtain in carrying out our experiments. We also recommend strongly that you read David Legge's *Introduction to Psychological Science* (A1) which will provide a background and theoretical orientation to the experiments described here.

Our approach

All experiments begin with some kind of problem or with some kind of question. Between the conceptualization of the question or the problem and the actual carrying out of the experiment the experimenter has to make a large number of decisions. The core of experimental design lies in the decision-making process which the experimenter goes through in setting up an experiment. The nature of the decisions involved, the basis upon which they are made, the constraints they impose and the implications which arise from them emerge in the context of our discussing how to set up each particular experiment. What we have tried to do is to give a 'guided tour' of how an experimenter, given a particular problem, might arrive at one particular experimental solution. By adopting this approach we have had in mind the value of relating the main principles of experimental design closely to concrete experimental problems. You will find a more abstract and systematic approach to experimental design in Steve Miller's text.

Part Two of our book contains eight 'set' experiments. We have used a standard format in describing each experiment and it would be as well at this point to outline the rationale underlying the format we have adopted. The first section, which we have called 'Theoretical background', deals with the conceptualization of the experimental problem. The experimental design and procedure are dealt with in the following 'Method' section. Then come two sections called 'Treatment of results' and 'Interpretation of results'. The first of these concerns scoring and analysing the data. All the analyses we suggest are dealt with fully in Steve Miller's text, and we assume that at this point in each experiment you will look up the relevant tests in Steve Miller's book. 'Interpretation of results' concerns how the data can be interpreted with regard to the initial experimental problem, and with the theoretical or practical implications of the results. The final section, which we call 'Discussion points', deals with some of the wider issues arising from the experiment, with special emphasis on problems of experimental design and interpretation.

In working through the experiments in Part Two, you will find that while the first four experiments concentrate more on problems of experimental design, the last four experiments involve a more 'sophisticated' and fuller treatment of theoretical issues. We have also, in the later experiments, included two which require the use of laboratory apparatus. Experiment 5 should be carried out using a piece of apparatus called a 'tachistoscope'. However, this experiment *can* also be carried out using an alternative method which does not involve that

15

apparatus. Experiment 6 can only be carried out by those of you who have access to standard reaction time equipment.

The final part of the book includes a resumé of some of the main points to be borne in mind when designing an experiment and some suggestions for further experiments for you to try.

Finally, just before we launch you into the first experiment, a word of caution. It is easier than you may think to rush into the testing phase of an experiment without being absolutely certain about what one is doing! What the experimenter does in the testing phase is described in each 'Method' section. You will probably find that this section needs to be read several times before you feel ready to go ahead with the experiment.

Part Two
First Experiments

Experiment 1
Measuring the apparent extent
of the Müller-Lyer illusion

1.1 Theoretical background

Figure 1 shows the Müller-Lyer illusion. The illusion arises out of the fact that, although the two straight lines between the 'arrow heads' and the 'fins' are the same length, most people tend to perceive the line between the 'arrow heads' as being much shorter.

The Müller-Lyer figure is one of a class of similar 'geometric' illusions. For this experiment we are going to assume that we have just discovered this illusion and that we want to find out something about what conditions affect the apparent extent, or size, of the illusion. That is, we are going to choose one particular independent variable to manipulate and determine whether or not it affects the apparent size of the illusion. This exemplifies one possible strategy by which psychological research proceeds. For example, we may test for the effects of a number of different independent variables on the apparent size of the illusion and find that some of these variables have no effect upon the apparent size of the illusion, while others do. Given such an outcome, we may hypothesize particular reasons

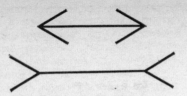

Fig. 1 *The Müller-Lyer illusion*

why particular variables have an effect and others do not, and go on to design experiments that put those ideas to the test.

For the present, however, and as a first step, we will make no theoretical assumptions at all. We will simply set out to determine whether or not a particular independent variable has any effect upon the apparent size of the illusion. We could choose, arbitrarily, any one of a number of independent variables to manipulate. You might like to think up some possible choices yourself, but let's pick one to exemplify the possibilities – that of orientation. In manipulating orientation, we could present the Müller-Lyer figure to subjects in the horizontal plane, in the vertical plane, or at any oblique orientation between these two. Let us choose only the two extreme possibilities, and compare the effects of presenting the illusion either horizontally or vertically. Our aim then, may be stated simply – we wish to discover whether or not there is any difference in the apparent extent of the Müller-Lyer illusion when presented vertically and when presented horizontally.

1.2 Method

Design
Our independent variable, then, is orientation, and our dependent variable is the apparent size of the Müller-Lyer figure. Given these choices, we now have to make a number of decisions with regard to the details of our experimental situation. How shall we measure the apparent extent? How many subjects do we need to test? How many readings do we need to obtain from each subject under each of the two conditions, horizontal and vertical presentation?

One major decision should, however, be taken before all these, and that is whether to use a between-subjects or a within-subjects design. Should we test all subjects under both the

18

horizontal and vertical presentation conditions, or should we test a different group of subjects under each of the two conditions? While there are advantages and disadvantages to each of these two alternatives, we could use either design here. We shall opt for the independent design, and choose a different group of subjects for each of our two conditions.

In essence then, we have decided on the simplest experimental design. We have chosen two levels (horizontal and vertical) of our independent variable (orientation) and will test the effects of these two conditions on our dependent variable (apparent extent of the Müller-Lyer figure). We have also decided, arbitrarily, that we will employ a different group of subjects in each of our two conditions.

Procedure

One technique for measuring the apparent extent of the Müller-Lyer illusion is to adopt the psychophysical method of adjustment. This method involves presenting the subject with the illusion such that one part of the figure remains the same, and the other part of the figure is variable. The subjects' task is to adjust the variable part of the figure until the two central lines appear to be the same length. Such a figure can be made easily from two pieces of white card or paper, as shown in Figure 2:

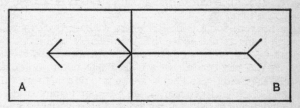

Fig. 2 *Adjustable Müller-Lyer figure*

The adjustable figure is presented to the subject such that the two central lines are obviously not equal in length. The subject's task is to adjust, by sliding in or out, part B of the figure until the two parts of the figure appear to be of equal length.

We now need to make some decision about the number of subjects to test, and also about the number of observations we need to obtain from each subject. If possible, one might test twelve subjects in each condition. The number is fairly arbitrary, but there are two constraints in deciding on the number. First, if we test too few, then any difference between the horizontal and vertical conditions might be 'swamped' by the individual differences between the subjects. If we test too many, however, the cost to ourselves is that the experiment is going to take a very long time to complete. Twelve subjects in each condition seems a reasonable compromise between these two considerations.

Similar considerations apply when we come to decide how many observations to obtain from each subject. One of the major characteristics of human performance is its variability. We need to obtain a sufficient number of observations from each subject to enable us to get a fair estimate of the average performance underlying each individual's variation. Twenty observations seems a reasonable number in order to do this, and it makes calculating the average fairly easy.

We have decided then, to test twelve subjects in each condition, and to obtain twenty observations from each subject. These numbers are not, of course, absolutely critical, and you can vary them depending on the circumstances in which you do the experiment. In a class or group context, the most obvious procedure is to 'double up' on experimenters and subjects. That is, half the group act as subjects under one condition, and also test the other half of the group as experimenters in the other condition.

In a between-subjects design where we have two groups of subjects being tested under the two different conditions, we want to be able to assume that any difference in *performance* between the two conditions is indeed due to the difference between the conditions. That is, we want to be able to attribute the effects on the dependent variable to our manipulation of the independent variable. What kinds of *other* variables might also lead to differences between our two conditions?

First, our two groups of subjects are likely to vary in a large number of individual ways, including intelligence, personality characteristics, motivation, and so on. How do we avoid biasing our experimental result because of such individual differences? We cannot, of course, *eliminate* such differences! What we *can* do, however, is to make quite sure that we decide which group our subjects are assigned to at *random*. This means that any one subject has an equal chance of being in either group, and that no *bias* enters into the way in which we decide

20

which group a subject will be in. It might seem, in a class situation, that the easiest way to do this might be to say that all those individuals in the front rows will be in one condition, all those in the back rows in the other condition. But does this remove any possibility of bias? If you think about it for a moment you'll probably see why it does not. Whether or not people tend to sit at the front or at the back of a class may well reflect personality characteristics, or motivational differences. That procedure of selecting groups may well lead to a *difference* between group results which has nothing to do with our independent variable. One general procedure for assigning subjects to groups is to use random number tables. If we went around the class using the random number tables, we could assign, for example, even numbers from the table for the horizontal condition and odd numbers for the vertical condition. As we want an *equal* number of subjects in each group however, we might have to adjust the group slightly at the end of this procedure. An even simpler alternative would be to use a 'lottery' procedure. We would need twelve small cards, or pieces of paper, marked with an H (horizontal) and twelve marked with a V (vertical). Then, having shuffled these thoroughly, and making quite sure no one can *see* what is on the card, each individual in the class 'draws' one card to decide which group he will be in.

The second source of variables which might bias our results is the testing situation itself. Obviously, we need to ensure that as far as possible, the subjects in each group are tested under identical circumstances. You can probably think of several aspects of the testing situation that might vary, and which need, therefore, to be controlled. Three of the most important are: first, the distance between the subject and the adjustable Müller-Lyer figure; second, whether the adjustable part of the figure is presented as larger or smaller than the constant part of the figure; and third, how long we allow the subject to take in adjusting the figure until the two parts appear to be equal. We'll now make some decisions on each of these points. As far as the distance between the subject and the adjustable figure is concerned, the best solution is to ensure that this distance is constant, for all subjects, in both conditions. This is done simply by marking a particular spot on the table at which the subject is sitting, and always making the subject adjust the figure at that spot. The subject should not be allowed to pick the figure up, for example, and move it closer. Second, we could also always present the adjustable figure so that the left-hand part of the figure is much longer than the constant part. Within this constraint, however, we can vary the actual length of the figure so that the actual length of the left-hand part is different each time. This can be done more or less 'haphazardly'. We don't need to measure the length of this part of the figure before presenting it to the subject. Lastly, what about the amount of time we allow the subject for adjusting the figure? This aspect of the situation we have, by definition, to leave up to the subject, since we have set his task as that of moving the left-hand part of the figure to and fro until the two parts of the figure appear to be of equal length. Although our subjects will undoubtedly vary the time they take to do this from one trial to another, there is no reason to believe that this variation should bias our results. That is, we have no reason to believe that, on average, subjects will take any longer to adjust the figure in the horizontal condition than in the vertical condition.

Having dealt with our selection of subjects into the two groups, and various aspects of the testing situation itself, we are nearly ready to begin to prepare the experiment. We need finally, however, to consider two more points in a little more detail: first, exactly how we're going to measure the apparent extent of the illusion; and second, how we're going to instruct our subjects.

The apparent extent of the illusion is given by the difference between the length of the constant part of the figure, and the length of the adjustable part of the figure after the subject has judged the two parts to be equal. After each judgement then, the experimenter must measure the length of the adjustable part of the figure and record it. Each experimenter should have a ruler with a centimetre scale on it, and a prepared scoring sheet with the numbers 1 to 20 written in a column down the sheet. After each judgement, he records on the sheet the actual length of the adjustable part of the figure in centimetres and millimetres. Also, the subject should not be able to see the measurements that the experimenter makes. If he did so, he might get some idea of how 'well' he was doing and so alter his judgements accordingly.

Our instructions to the subjects are implicit in the procedure, and are fairly straightforward. We need to tell the subject that he will be presented with the illusion figure and that his task is simply to adjust the figure until the two parts appear to be of equal length. Since the subject may well already be familiar with the illusion, it may be necessary to stress that his task is to judge the *apparent* equality of the two parts of the figure, and *not* to try to 'compensate' for the illusion.

1.3 Treatment of results

At the end of the experiment as described, we will have obtained twenty measures of apparent extent from twelve subjects under each of our two conditions. Our first task will be to obtain the average, or mean value, of apparent extent for each subject. This we do simply by adding the twenty measurements for each subject separately and dividing the result by twenty. The mean values obtained in this way give us the actual length of the adjustable part of the figure. To obtain the apparent extent of the illusion we have to compare the actual lengths as judged by the subjects, with the length of the constant part of the figure. For each subject then, we subtract the mean length of the adjustable part of the figure from the length of the constant part of the figure. Suppose, for one subject, the mean value obtained was 3·4 centimetres and we had constructed the figure such that the length of the constant part of it was 5·0 centimetres. The apparent extent of the illusion, for that subject, would then be 1·6 centimetres. In this way we can determine, for each subject under both conditions, the apparent extent of the illusion figure, and having done this we can tabulate the results of the experiment as shown in Table 1.

Having tabulated these mean values we are now in a position to inspect the results of the experiment. Looking at the results, however, there will be a fair amount of variation between the different values and it is unlikely that we will be able to tell whether or not there is any overall difference between the two conditions. We need a summary of the results which will at least give us some better indication as to whether or not our two conditions differ, so we must next complete the table by calculating the overall mean value under each condition. Having done this, we can now state the general result of the experiment. Suppose we find that the apparent extent of the illusion is 1·2 centimetres under the vertical condition and 1·6 centimetres under the horizontal condition. Certainly, two such values suggest that the apparent extent of the illusion is greater when the illusion is horizontal. How do we know that

Table 1 Apparent extent of the Müller-Lyer illusion presented in the vertical and horizontal positions

Horizontal presentation		Vertical presentation	
Subject: 1		Subject: 13	
2		14	
3		15	
4		16	
5		17	
6		18	
7		19	
8		20	
9		‚21	
10		22	
11		23	
12		24	
Σ		Σ	
$\bar{x}$		$\bar{x}$	

this is a 'real' difference? Until we analyse our data statistically, we don't, so our next task is to select and carry out an appropriate statistical analysis.

In selecting the appropriate statistical analysis we have to consider two principal points: first, the design of our experiment, and second, the kind of data we have obtained. Our design is a between-subjects design with two conditions. Appropriate tests for this design are the Mann-Whitney U-test and the unrelated t-test (A8, Ch. 4). Our data fit the requirements for the use of parametric tests, so we should, ideally, use the unrelated t-test to analyse our data.

Before evaluating the results of the t-test we have to consider the nature of the hypothesis of the experiment in order to determine whether a one- or two-tailed test is appropriate. We did not discuss hypotheses as such in describing the experiment. We did, however, decide to test whether or not there would be any difference in the apparent extent of the illusion when presented vertically and when presented horizontally. Our prediction, or our experimental hypothesis, is, therefore, that there will be a difference between the two conditions. But we have no reason to expect the apparent extent of the illusion to be greater for the horizontal condition, or for the vertical. Thus we are dealing here with a two-tailed test.

24

The experiment had two possible outcomes. Either orientation (horizontal *v.* vertical) affected the apparent extent of the Müller-Lyer illusion or it did not. The experiment was designed solely to determine whether or not one particular independent variable, orientation, had any effect upon our dependent variable. We can assume that any difference in the performance of our two groups of subjects is due to our manipulation of the independent variable. We cannot, however, make any conclusion as to why orientation affects the apparent extent of the illusion, since we had no initial reason to suppose that it should. If indeed we have found an effect due to orientation, all we can conclude is that any explanation of the illusion will have to take that fact into account. Similarly, if we have found *no* effect due to orientation, we can at least conclude that any explanation of the illusion which would lead us to expect such an effect may be wrong.

1.5 Discussion points

The most obvious and striking feature of this, your first experiment, is probably the very large number of points one has to consider, and decisions one has to make in setting up an experiment. Having chosen the variables to be investigated, many of the decisions that had to be made subsequently had one major aim only – that of 'control'. By control we mean steps that have to be taken in order to ensure that any differences we obtain in our dependent variable can be attributed to our manipulation of the independent variable *and to no other variable*. If we fail to control the experimental situation in this way, we run the considerable risk of claiming that particular independent variables have an effect on our dependent variable when this is not the case. That is why we took care to ensure that our subjects were assigned at random to our two groups, that all subjects were given the same instructions, and that the actual testing situation was the same for subjects in each group. This principle of control is fundamental to good experimental design, and we shall meet it again in every experiment in this book.

Two other features of the present experiment are worth commenting on here. First, we employed the minimum number of 'conditions' – that is, two. If we wish to determine whether or not an independent variable has any effect on our dependent variable, then we have to pick at least two different levels (or conditions) in our independent variable in order to do so. We could not have investigated the effects of orientation on the apparent extent of the Müller-Lyer illusion if we had presented *all* subjects with the illusion in the horizontal plane! Most of the experiments we describe subsequently involve only two or three conditions of one independent variable.

Second, we used a between-subjects design – that is, we had a different group of subjects in each of our two conditions. We could also have chosen to use a within-subjects design in this experiment, by testing the *same* subjects in each of our two conditions. In the present experiment our choice of a between-subjects design was arbitrary. There are, however, advantages and disadvantages associated with each basic type of design. We will mention just one here. You will have noticed the considerable amount of variability in the data you collected in this experiment. Not surprisingly, quite a large part of this variability is due to the individual differences that exist between subjects. If we use a within-subjects design, in which each subject serves under both conditions, then the effects of this individual variation will be the *same* for each condition. To put it another way, so far as individual differences are concerned, each subject, in a within-subjects design, acts as his own control. On these grounds, we might expect a within-subjects design to be more *sensitive* to the effects of any particular independent variable. However, a within-subjects design involves, by definition, a certain amount of *repeated* testing, across at least two conditions. The effect of repeated testing can itself lead to problems in experimental design and control. Some of these problems are dealt with in our next experiment, which is about solving anagrams and which uses a within-subjects design.

Experiment 2
Solving anagrams of common and uncommon words

2.1 Theoretical background

'Word frequency' refers to how common or uncommon a particular word is in written English. It's easy to get some intuitive feel for word frequency – compare 'cat', for example, with 'gnu', or 'trice' with 'mice'. It's also possible to obtain an objective 'word count' by sampling passages of written English and noting how frequently each particular word is used. The best known word count was produced in this way by Thorndike and Lorge (1944). Word frequency has been shown to affect performance in a variety of experimental tasks. It is much easier, for example, to learn a list of common unrelated words than to learn a list of uncommon words. In studies of recognition threshold it has been found that it takes longer to recognize uncommon words than it does common words. The aim of the present experiment is to determine whether or not word frequency affects performance in solving anagrams.

Why should word frequency affect anagram solution? Try solving these two anagrams: AHSPE; LABTE. Most of you will probably come up with the solutions SHAPE and TABLE. We suspect that few of you will have thought of PHASE and BLEAT. (If you've read this far *before* solving the anagrams, try them on someone else!) Phase and bleat are, of course, less common words than shape and table. Consider how one might set about the problem of solving an anagram. One strategy might be to rearrange several of the letters and then attempt to think up words that 'fit' that combination. Many words begin with the letters SH, for example, and given that combination of letters you might 'generate' the word shape, and then check that it fits with the remaining letters of the anagram. If generating possible solution words in this way plays any part in anagram solving, then we might well expect word frequency to affect anagram solution. This is because, in any 'free responding' situation which requires subjects simply to generate words, more common words are produced than uncommon words, and the common words tend to be produced before the uncommon words. If, for example, subjects were asked to free associate to the word ANIMAL, the chances are that 'cat' would be produced before 'gnu', and though most people would think of 'cat', many people would not think of 'gnu' at all. Our aim is to design an experiment which will determine whether or not word frequency affects anagram solution. Our expectations in this case, however, are more specific than that. We expect that subjects will do better in solving anagrams of common words than they will in solving anagrams of uncommon words.

2.2 Method

Design

Our independent variable is word frequency and our two conditions are common and uncommon solution words. We have also decided to use a within-subjects design – that is, we will present each of our subjects with anagrams of both common and uncommon words. How many anagrams should we present? If we present too few, we run the risk of not obtaining sufficient data to give us a good measure of each subject's average performance in solving the anagrams. If we present too many, on the other hand, the 'cost' to ourselves is that the experiment will take much longer to do than it need. Within these constraints, eighteen seems as good a number as any, so we will present each subject with nine anagrams of common words, and nine anagrams of uncommon words. The anagram solution words are in Appendix I. They should not, of course, be seen by the subject until after the experiment has been completed.

We next have to consider those aspects of the experimental situation which need to be 'controlled'. Our prediction is that anagrams of uncommon words will be more difficult to solve than anagrams of common words. What other variables might affect anagram solution difficulty? One obvious possibility is the length of the solution words. It is more difficult to solve anagrams of long words than anagrams of short words. We can control for this variable by ensuring that all our solution words, both common and uncommon, are the same length. In fact, we have already done this, as all the words in Appendix I are five letters long.

A second variable which will affect the difficulty of solving an anagram is the extent to which the letters of the solution word are rearranged in constructing the anagram. For example, compare these two anagrams: HFESL; FSHEL. In the first anagram, not one of the five letters is in the correct order for the solution word. In the second, all the letters are in the correct order except the F. We can control for this variable by using the same rearrangement of letters for both our common and our uncommon words. If we number the five letters of a solution word '1, 2, 3, 4, 5', for example, we could construct an anagram by rearranging the letters into the order, '3, 5, 4, 1, 2'. We can then use this rearrangement for both an uncommon and a common solution word.

We cannot, however, construct *all* our anagrams using exactly the same rearrangement of letters. If we did that, our subjects might well, after solving a few anagrams, learn how to solve the rest by discovering the way in which we had constructed the anagrams! To prevent this happening, we will need to use a number of different rearrangements in constructing our anagrams. We will suggest some possible rearrangements in the following section.

Having dealt with variables other than word frequency which might also affect anagram solution difficulty, we turn now to consider some of the implications of using a within-subjects design. In this case, we are presenting each subject with nine anagrams of common words, and nine anagrams of uncommon words. What might the effects of such repeated testing be? One possibility is that, through practice at solving successive anagrams, our subjects get better and better at the task. The more experience our subjects have at solving the anagrams, the more they will learn about how to solve anagrams. A second possibility is that, while at the beginning of the experiment subjects may begin solving anagrams with some enthusiasm, as the task continues and more anagrams are presented they become increasingly disenchanted and bored with the task. These kinds of possibility have serious consequences with regard to the order in which we present our two conditions.

Suppose we took what seems to be a fairly obvious and easy order of presentation of our two conditions, and presented our subjects with the nine anagrams of common words first, and then the nine anagrams of uncommon words afterwards. Suppose also, that we have a subject who starts the experiment enthusiastically but becomes increasingly bored with the task as we continue to present one anagram after another. That will mean that this subject will do much worse in solving the uncommon word anagrams, which we have presented after the common ones, than he would have if we had presented the uncommon ones first, before he had become bored! Suppose we had another 'contrary' subject who substantially improves his ability to solve anagrams through practice at solving them. This subject will do much better at the uncommon word anagrams, if we present them after the common ones, than he would have done if we had presented them first.

Obviously these kinds of 'order effect' are going to distort our results. We may obtain differences between our two conditions which are due not to our independent variable (word frequency) but to the order in which we have presented the two conditions. So we have to take such order effects into account in designing our experiment. How can we do this? Well, we cannot possibly *eliminate* the effects of repeated testing. We cannot prevent our subjects from improving their performance through practice or from becoming increasingly 'fatigued' as the experiment proceeds. What we can do, however, is to ensure that such order effects do not *bias* the outcome of the experiment. That is, we can ensure that such order effects have a more or less *equal* effect upon each of our two conditions.

Perhaps the most obvious way of achieving this would be simply to present half our subjects with the uncommon word anagrams before the common ones, and the other half of our subjects with the common word anagrams before the uncommon ones. Thus, any order effects should, on average, balance out between the two conditions. This procedure will not do here, however. If we present all the common and uncommon word anagrams blocked together, our subjects after solving a few anagrams of each kind, will learn the frequency of the solution words for that block. This means that, in generating possible solution words for the anagram, the subjects will know whether the required word is common or uncommon.

For this reason, we will adopt another technique to control for order effects, and that is to randomize completely the order in which we present uncommon and common word anagrams to each subject. We can do this quite easily if we put each anagram separately on one blank card, and then 'shuffle' the cards before testing each subject. By randomizing our presentation order in this way, we ensure that there will be no systematic bias in our results due to the order in which we present our two conditions.

30

Finally, we conclude this section by giving some thought to our choice of *dependent* variable. How are we going to measure how difficult particular anagrams are to solve? Perhaps the best index of difficulty is simply how long it takes the subject to solve the anagram. So, we shall measure anagram solution time, and we expect, of course, that anagrams of uncommon words will take longer to solve than will anagrams of common words. It is also possible that our subjects will take a very long time indeed to solve some of the anagrams, and may come to feel that there *is* no solution! To prevent distressing our subjects unduly in this way, we will impose a time limit of 3 minutes, after which, if the subject has not solved a particular anagram, we will go on and present the next one. The choice of a 3 minute limit is fairly arbitrary. Imposing a time limit also means that we have introduced a *second* dependent variable, and that is the number of anagrams which subjects can solve within the time allowed. Again, our prediction leads us to expect that subjects will, within the time limit, solve fewer anagrams of uncommon words than anagrams of common words.

Procedure

We can run this experiment in two ways, depending on individual circumstances. In a class or group setting, half the group could act as experimenters and test the other half of the group as subjects. Alternatively, one experimenter only can test the subjects individually. About ten subjects would be ideal, though of course there is no reason why more should not be tested.

The experimenter's first task will be to prepare the anagrams. Using the words given in Appendix I, nine anagrams of common words and nine of uncommon words can be constructed using the following letter rearrangements:

$$
\begin{array}{ccccc}
1, & 3, & 2, & 5, & 4 \\
2, & 5, & 3, & 1, & 4 \\
4, & 3, & 1, & 2, & 5 \\
3, & 5, & 1, & 2, & 4 \\
5, & 2, & 1, & 4, & 3 \\
1, & 2, & 5, & 4, & 3 \\
3, & 4, & 5, & 1, & 2 \\
2, & 3, & 4, & 1, & 5 \\
4, & 5, & 1, & 2, & 3 \\
\end{array}
$$

The order 1, 2, 3, 4, 5 corresponds to the actual solution word, and the rearrangements given above range from fairly easy to more difficult ones, depending on the number of letters in the anagram which retain their correct position in the solution word. Each rearrangement is used twice, once for a common word, and once for an uncommon word. Each anagram should be printed in block capitals on a separate white card or sheet of paper.

The experimenter should number each anagram from 1

Table 2 Solution times for anagrams of common and uncommon words

		Subjects									
		1	2	3	4	5	6	7	8	9	10
Common words:											
1	___	9									
2	___	18									
3	___	120									
4	___	4									
5	___	2									
6	___	–									
7	___	65									
8	___	32									
9	___	3									
Uncommon words:											
10	___	15									
11	___	92									
12	___	170									
13	___	–									
14	___	110									
15	___	–									
16	___	86									
17	___	49									
18		–									

through to 18 so that he can keep track of the subject's solution attempts and knows what the correct solution word is. To this end, it would be a good idea for the experimenter to have the data sheet prepared beforehand, as shown in Table 2.

The experimenter can enter the actual solution words down the left-hand column of the table. As the experiment proceeds, he can enter each solution time in the column headed 'subject'. Remember that the order in which the subject receives each anagram is *not* the order in which the solution word is entered into the table. Having the data sheet prepared in this way, and each anagram numbered from 1 to 18, ensures that the experimenter always knows which anagram the subject is attempting and can enter the solution time in the appropriate space. Where subjects fail to solve the anagram in the 3 minutes allowed, the experimenter can leave the appropriate space unfilled.

The experimenter will need either a stop watch or a wrist watch with an accurate second hand in order to measure anagram solution times. These times should be measured in seconds, to the nearest whole second.

The subjects should be instructed that they are going to be presented with a number of anagrams and that they will be allowed 3 minutes to attempt to solve each one. As soon as they think they know the solution word they should say the word aloud. If the word they think of is not the correct solution word, the experimenter will tell them so and they can continue to try to solve the anagram until either they get the solution word or the 3 minutes time limit is up.

The experimenter should sit facing the subject and arrange the materials so that he can easily time from the moment he presents each anagram to the subject till the subject produces the correct solution word. The experimenter must also ensure that the subject does not see each anagram until the experimenter actually lays it in front of him. Also, of course, the subject should not be able to see the experimenter's data sheet. The subject should not be told how long he takes to solve each anagram until the experimenter has finished testing him. Finally, before testing each subject, the experimenter should shuffle the anagrams thoroughly.

2.3 Treatment of results

After you have completed the testing of your subject in this experiment, the data will have been entered in Table 2. We are not particularly interested here in how long it took particular subjects to solve particular anagrams. We are interested in how well our subjects coped with anagrams of uncommon words compared with common words. There are two types of data: the solution times, in seconds, and the number of anagrams which were solved. Examining the data, the first point to note is that the number of solution times we have measured is often much less than the possible total of eighteen per subject. Moreover, there probably seem to be fewer solution times for the uncommon words than for the common words. In this kind of situation, the mean average may not be the best way of summarizing the data. This is because the mean is affected quite substantially by extreme scores. Consider these two sets of scores, for example:

(a) 5, 7, 6, 5, 4, 3
(b) 6, 3, 5, 4, 7, 29

Apart from the one score of 29, the two sets of figures are very similar. The means of the two, however, are quite different: 5 for set (a), but 9 for set (b). In this case, the median, or middle score, is the better measure of 'central tendency', and in fact, the median is $5\frac{1}{2}$ for both sets of scores. In our solution time data, wherever subjects failed to solve an anagram, the solution time score, in effect, is 180 seconds or more. Treating such cases as if the solution time *was* 180 seconds, determine the median solution time for each subject, for each condition. In our fictitious data for Subject 1 in Table 2, for example, the median solution times are 18 seconds for the common words and 110 seconds for the uncommon words – in each case, the middle or fifth highest score. Also, for each subject in each condition, add up the number of anagrams which the subject failed to solve. These two sets of data can now be entered in a table ready for analysis similar to the one shown in Table 3.

From our table of results we can now summarize the outcome of the experiment by obtaining the mean solution times, and the mean numbers of anagrams unsolved, in each condition.

Our next task, of course, is to analyse these data in order to determine whether or not the differences between the means we have obtained are statistically significant. A very quick test to apply, separately for solution times and for the number of anagrams unsolved, is the Sign test. The Sign test, however, only takes the *direction* of the differences into account, and ignores the size of the difference. We would probably, therefore, want to apply more sensitive tests to these data. We would be fairly safe in assuming that our solution time data are appropriately analysed by a parametric test. Since we have a two-condition, within-subjects design, we can use the related

Table 3 Median solution times and number of anagrams solved, for common and uncommon words

	Median solution times (secs)		Numbers unsolved	
	Common words	Uncommon words	Common words	Uncommon words
Subject: 1	18	110	1	3
2				
3				
4				
5				
6				
7				
8				
9				
10				
Σ				
x̄				

t-test on these data. In the case of our 'numbers unsolved' data, however, a parametric test will not be appropriate, and for these data we will use the Wilcoxon test, (A8, Chapter 5) rather than the *t*-test.

In determining the probabilities for our statistical results, we must remember that our hypothesis in this experiment is one-tailed. Unlike the situation in our previous experiment, our prediction here was that anagrams of uncommon words would be more difficult to solve. Specifically, we were expecting longer solution times for uncommon word anagrams than for common ones, and more unsolved anagrams for uncommon than common words. Not only were we simply predicting *a* difference between our two conditions; we were predicting the specific *direction* of the difference. In such cases, our statistical test is one-tailed.

2.4 Interpretation of results

The results of this experiment should clearly support the hypothesis that subjects find anagrams of uncommon words more difficult to solve than those of common words. The experiment demonstrates, therefore, that word frequency does indeed affect performance in anagram solving. This conclusion depends, of course, on our assuming that the outcome of your statistical tests enabled you to reject the null hypothesis – that is, the hypothesis that the mean for the uncommon word anagrams is not greater than the mean for the common word anagrams. It is also possible that the results of the statistical tests do not enable you to reject the null hypothesis, in which case the only conclusion you can draw from the results is that the experiment provided no support for the notion that word frequency affects performance in an anagram solution task. We are, however, fairly confident that your results will demonstrate the predicted effect!

Though the experiment shows that word frequency does affect performance in solving anagrams, it does not tell us why or how this should be so. In section 2.1 we suggested that, in solving anagrams, one might look at various combinations of the letters and attempt to generate words which 'fit' the entire sequence of letters. We also pointed out that, since it is known that common words are more likely to be produced in a free responding situation than are uncommon words, this implied that subjects were likely to 'hit upon' the solution of uncommon word anagrams sooner than common ones. Our results, certainly, may be in line with this suggested explanation. But that is all. They do *not* 'prove' that this indeed is *how* people solve anagrams, or that this is *why* word frequency affects the ease or difficulty with which people do solve anagrams. This is an important point concerning the interpretation of experimental data. This experiment has demonstrated a psychological fact. That is, it has shown that variable *A* (word frequency) affects variable *B* (solution times in anagram solving). Our interpretation of why this should be so remains, on the basis of our data here, essentially speculative. Later on, we will discuss how experiments can be designed to test the correctness of alternative explanations of facts. For the present, however, we are concerned only with showing how experiments 'produce' facts, facts which we can add to our general knowledge of human behaviour as experimental psychologists.

2.5 Discussion points

A psychological fact is very often of the kind described above – that is, that variable *A* affects variable *B*. A psychological fact is also a statement of probability and not a statement of certainty. But that state of affairs is not peculiar to psychology. All branches of science are in the business of discovering and explaining observable facts, and *all* facts are logically uncertain and unproven. How do we select 'facts'? One way is to examine degrees of probability. In psychology, by convention only, we accept as a fact any event which could only occur, by chance, five times out of a hundred or less. This is the meaning of 'level of significance' in a statistical test. The function of a statistical test is to tell us how likely it is that the particular event we have observed occurred by chance. If it seems highly unlikely that the event could have occurred by chance, then we conclude that it is due to the operation of some systematic variable (our independent variable). Thus facts are statements to the effect that it is extremely unlikely that particular events could have occurred by chance. This is true of psychology; it is also the principle upon which engineers build bridges, architects design houses, or shipbuilders build ships.

Although we accept, by convention, that if the changes that occur in our dependent variable are very unlikely to be attributable to chance, then we can attribute those changes to our manipulation of the independent variable, we shall, of course, sometimes be wrong. This is why it is good practice to replicate experiments. 'Replicate' here means simply repeating the experiment. If several experimenters, carrying out the same experimental procedure quite independently, obtain similar results, then our confidence in the *reliability* of the effect obtained in the experiment increases. We may also wish to replicate a previous experiment but make some slight procedural changes in so doing. One reason for doing this is to determine the generality of the results obtained. If, for example, we find that in learning a list of words, individuals tend to remember the most recently presented words better than words experienced earlier, we may wish to determine whether or not this finding is also true for other types of material, such as letters or digits. In Experiment 3 we give an example of the value of replicating a previous experiment.

One other general point is worth emphasizing here, and that is the importance of controlling for the effects of repeated testing. In most psychology experiments we test each subject more than once. We have to be very careful to design our experiments such that the effects of repeated testing do not bias our results. In seeking to attribute the changes we observe in our dependent variable to the effects of our independent variable, we have to try to take into account all the other possible factors that might also lead to changes in our dependent variable.

Experiment 3
Recognizing letters presented to the right and to the left of the visual field

3.1 Theoretical background

When we first learn to read and write, we learn that letters and words are arranged in a left-to-right direction. Indeed, it may come as something of a surprise when, later on, we learn that this arrangement is not true for all languages. This left-to-right sequence means that, in reading, the information to be processed is, in effect, presented to the right of our visual field. If our reading habits have any permanent effect upon the way our visual perception is organized, then it follows that we should be able to recognize verbal material more easily when it is presented to the right of our visual field than when it is presented to the left of our visual field.

This notion may be tested by measuring what is called peripheral recognition. Peripheral recognition can be demonstrated quite easily. First, you need to fixate upon a point in the centre of your visual field. If you're sitting at a desk or at a table, put a 'marker' of some kind (for example, a blank piece of paper with an X in the middle of it) in the centre straight in front of your line of vision. This marker will serve as the fixation point. Fixating means concentrating your gaze exclusively on the marker and not allowing your eyes to move away from it either to the left or to the right. After a few moments of fixation on the marker you will need to 'rest' your eyes by allowing them to move (or closing them for a moment) otherwise you will find that your vision becomes blurred or you may start 'seeing double'. It is quite difficult to keep your vision exclusively focused on the fixation point for more than a few seconds, but we can only measure peripheral recognition when the eyes are fixated in this way. Having tried this out, next write down a word (any word) on another piece of paper and, while fixating on the central point, move the word slowly along the table in a straight line to the right of the fixation point. After a while you will find that you can no longer read the word. Repeat this procedure but now moving the word to the left of the fixation point. If you do not, in each case, reach a place where you can no longer read the word, one of two things has probably happened. First, you may be sitting a bit too far away from the fixation point. If that is so, move a bit closer and try again! Second, you may be allowing your eyes to move away from the fixation point as you move the word. And if that is so, try again, but this time being very careful to keep your eyes focused exclusively on the fixation point.

Using this procedure we are, in effect, obtaining a measure of peripheral recognition. Our measure of peripheral recognition is that distance from the fixation point at which the word can no longer be read. This distance is a measure of recognition *threshold* – that is, the point along some physical continuum at which we can identify the stimulus, in the sense of being able to name it correctly. Thresholds are discussed more fully in Experiment 5. For the present, the point to note is that a low threshold, implying greater sensitivity, is associated with increase in distance from the fixation point. That is, if our left-to-right reading habits lead to any permanent change in our perceptual organization, we would expect a lower recognition threshold (i.e. a *greater* distance from the fixation point) for words presented from the right of the visual field than for those presented from the left.

Using a procedure similar to that described above, Mishkin and Forgays (1952) carried out an experiment which showed, indeed that words presented to the right of the visual field were recognized more easily than words presented to left of the visual field. Words were recognized at a greater distance to the right of the visual field than to the left. This result suggests that our reading habits do lead to some permanent changes in our perceptual organization. This finding bears on the general theoretical issue concerning the extent to which the organization of perception is largely innate, rather than being determined largely through our perceptual experiences. The Gestalt psychologists had argued that perceptual organization was largely innate, and consequently influenced very little by our experience. Hebb (1949), in his *Organization of Behaviour*, attacked this viewpoint and argued that perceptual organization was acquired as a result of the interaction between the organism and his environment. The results obtained by Mishkin and Forgays clearly favour Hebb's view rather than the view of the Gestalt psychologists.

In the present experiment, we are going to attempt to replicate the study by Mishkin and Forgays. The general value of replicating previous studies was discussed in section 2.5. The particular reason for wishing to replicate the Mishkin and Forgays study is that their result might have been due to an artefact of their experimental design, rather than being due to any *real* difference in recognition thresholds for items presented to the right and to the left of the visual field. This artefact concerns the nature of words themselves. Consider the situation in which one presents the subject with a word to the left of the fixation point, and, at the same time, a word to the right of the fixation point. If these two words are at the same distance from the fixation point, and just far enough from it so that the subject can read a few of the letters in each case, but not the whole word, which word is the subject likely to be able to read first? The letters the subject can see in the word to the left of the fixation point are the last few letters of the word. Obviously, the first few letters of a word provide more information about what the word is likely to be than do the last few letters. For this reason alone, subjects may be able to recognize words more easily to the right of the visual field than to the left. The purpose of our replication, then, is to determine whether or not the results obtained by Mishkin and Forgays may have been attributable to this artefact rather than being due to any real differences in recognition thresholds to the right and to the left of the visual field.

To achieve this we will need to test recognition thresholds using stimuli which are symmetrical about the vertical axis, so that the same amount of information is given when only half the stimulus can be perceived from either the right or the left of the visual field. This is the case, for example, in the following geometric shapes:

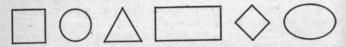

It is also the case in certain letters of the alphabet, such as

A, H, O, T and Y. In fact, there are eleven letters in the alphabet which – when printed in upper case – are symmetrical about the vertical axis. For this reason, and since letter recognition seems more akin to reading than does shape recognition, we will replicate the Mishkin and Forgays study using capital letters as our stimulus material.

Before going on to discuss the design of our replication, let us briefly consider the implications of the two most likely outcomes of our study. First, we may find that we obtain similar results to those obtained by Mishkin and Forgays. That is, we may find that capital letters are recognized more easily when presented to the right of the visual field than when presented to the left. Such an outcome implies that the results obtained by Mishkin and Forgays cannot be attributed – at least entirely – to the fact that the initial letters of a word convey more information about that word than do the last few letters. Alternatively, we may find that, using capital letters instead of words, there are no differences in recognition thresholds on the right and on the left of the visual field. This latter outcome implies that the Mishkin and Forgays results were an artefact of their use of words as the stimulus material.

Our aim is to measure recognition thresholds for capital letters presented to the left and to the right of the visual field. If reading habits have some permanent effect upon perceptual organization, then we would expect that letters presented to the right of the visual field will be recognized more easily than those presented to the left. If, on the other hand, reading habits do not affect perceptual organization, then letters presented to the left of the visual field should be recognized just as easily as those presented to the right.

3.2 Method

Design
Our two conditions are presentation to the left and presentation to the right of the visual field. For the reasons outlined in the previous section we will use symmetrical capital letters as the stimulus material. If we omit the letter I, the ten such letters remaining are as follows:

A H M O T U V W X Y

If we use all ten letters as our stimuli, we shall obtain a

41

reasonable number of observations on which to base an average. The choice of ten rather than eleven letters is simply to make calculating the mean average easier.

The next decision to be made is whether we should use a between-subjects or a within-subjects design. We have had some experience of each of the designs in the two previous experiments. One of the advantages of the within-subjects design, which we discussed earlier, is that each subject 'acts as his own control.' In section 3.1 we suggested that you try out fixating on a central point on a table in front of you, and moving a word on a piece of paper to the left and to the right of your visual field. From that demonstration, it will have been clear that the distance from the fixation point at which you could no longer read the word depended, among other things, on how close you were to the fixation point. The distance between the subject and the fixation point is one of the 'nuisance variables' which we will have to control. Controlling this particular variable is perhaps more easily achieved using a within-subjects design. In this case, so long as each individual subject is the same distance from the fixation point when letters are presented to the left and to the right of the visual field, then it does not matter if the distance from the fixation point varies between different subjects. Consider what this implies with respect to the values of our recognition threshold data. For a subject *very* close to the fixation point, the absolute values of our thresholds (that is, the distance between the fixation point and the point at which the subject can first read the letter) will be relatively small. Conversely, if the subject is farther away from the fixation point, the values of our thresholds will be relatively large. Using a within-subjects design these absolute values are not important, since we have eliminated the possibility of bias due to this particular nuisance variable by ensuring that the distance between the fixation point and the subject is constant for each subject separately. If we use a between-subjects design, we would have to ensure that that distance was constant for *all* subjects.

One other potential nuisance variable is the different characteristics of individual subjects' eyesight. Some of our subjects may, for example, be slightly long-sighted or slightly short-sighted. Differences of this kind will create problems if, as in a between-subjects design, we have to ensure that the distance between the subject and the fixation point is constant for all subjects.

There are other possible reasons for preferring to use a within-subjects design in the present experiment. The two examples described above serve to illustrate the kinds of considerations which may lead an experimenter to opt for one design rather than the other. In summary, we will be presenting each subject with the ten capital letters to the right and to the left of the visual field, whilst the subject fixates on the central point. Obviously, we will have to present each of the ten letters separately once to the left and once to the right of the visual field. The different letters may themselves differ in ease of recognition, and for that reason it would not do to, say, present one set of five under one condition and the remaining five under the other condition.

The choice of a within-subjects design means that, as in the previous experiment, we have to be particularly careful to control for the effects of repeated testing. In the present experiment, we need to consider the order in which we present particular letters, and also the order in which we present the two conditions (to the left and to the right of the visual field). One solution is to randomize completely the order in which each letter is presented within each condition, and to alternate between presentation to the left and presentation to the right of the visual field. Thus, each subject will be presented alternately with a letter to the right and to the left of the visual field until each letter has been presented once to each side.

Procedure

As before, this experiment can be run in a class context or on an individual basis. The choice of the number of subjects to test is determined as much by the availability of subjects as any other consideration. Since we will obtain ten observations from each subject under each condition, ten or twelve subjects would be a good number to test. While one could test fewer subjects, bear in mind that the smaller the sample size, the greater the risk that the sample may be biased and not representative of the population. Also, of course, with small numbers of subjects, any differences between the two conditions are less likely to give a significant result in the statistical analysis.

The experimenter's first task will be to prepare the stimulus material and to prepare a scoring sheet for recording the data. The stimulus letters can each be printed in capitals on separate pieces of white card or paper. It will be better to make these of uniform size so far as possible, though without going to the lengths of measuring the letters up. The same ten stimuli should be used under each of the two conditions, so that any discrepancies in the printing of the letters are constant under each condition. A suitable scoring sheet is illustrated in Table 4.

Table 4 Distance from fixation point for letter recognition to the right and to the left of the visual field

| | | Visual field | | | | | | | | | | | | | | | | | | | | | |
| | Left | | | | | | | | | | Right | | | | | | | | | | |
Subject:	1	2	3	4	5	6	7	8	9	10	Subject:	1	2	3	4	5	6	7	8	9	10
Letter: A											Letter: A										
H											H										
M											M										
O											O										
T											T										
U											U										
V											V										
W											W										
X											X										
Y											Y										
Σ											Σ										
x̄											x̄										

In Table 4 the letters are placed in alphabetic sequence, for ease of scoring, though of course the letters will be presented in a random order to each subject. Prior to testing each subject, the experimenter should 'shuffle' the ten letters twice, and make a note separately of the two random orders so generated. One of the two orders can, arbitrarily, be used for presentation to the left of the visual field, and the other for presentation to the right. On a further card, or piece of paper, the experimenter should also put a small filled circle, or some similar mark, to serve as the fixation point.

We consider next the procedure for presenting the stimulus material and for measuring the recognition threshold. The subject should be seated at a table facing the experimenter. At the centre of the table in front of the subject, the fixation point should be placed. The experimenter will need a tape measure (or metric rule, if available) and this should be laid on the table a little behind the fixation point, and such that the measurements on the tape (or rule) are facing the experimenter. The general arrangement is depicted in Figure 3.

If using a metre rule, the fixation point should be in line with the centre of the rule. If using a tape measure, line the fixation point up with some convenient value, such as 20 or 30 inches. To achieve the best arrangement for testing the experimenter will need to obtain some 'pilot' data. Using a few letters *not* included in the set of ten to be presented later, ask one or two subjects to fixate on the fixation point and, by

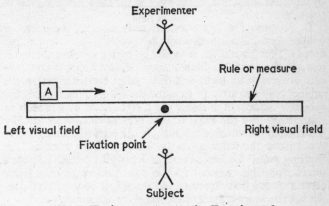

Fig. 3 *Testing arrangement for Experiment 3*

slowly moving each letter from the extreme right and left of the visual field towards the centre, roughly determine when the subject can read out the letter correctly. If the subject can do this even when the letters are at the extreme ends of the rule or measure, you will need to adjust the positioning depicted in Figure 3 accordingly, by – for example – decreasing the distance between the subject and the fixation point. Note that, as experimenter, you will be presenting a letter to the subject's *left* visual field when you present it from your *right*, and vice versa. When scoring the data in Table 4, it is important not to confuse the experimenter's 'left' with the subject's 'left'.

Having determined an optimal testing arrangement, we turn now to the details of the presentation procedure. In the demonstration we discussed in section 3.1 we suggested that you move the word away from the fixation point until you could no longer read it. The drawback to this procedure is, of course, that you knew what the word was even when you could no longer read it. So we will present each letter from the extreme

45

sides of the measure or rule, and bring it towards the centre. The subject's task is to call out the name of the letter as soon as he thinks he can read it. Our measure is the distance between the centre of our rule, or tape, and the place at which the subject reads the letter name correctly. The distance should be read off from the centre of the letter in each case, and it might be easier to do this if the centre of the letter is marked by a dot, or small line, at the edge of the card which is next to the tape or rule.

If we move the letter continuously towards the centre it will be very difficult to control the speed at which the letter is moved. For this reason, it would be better to move the letter towards the centre in discrete steps of, say, half a centimetre, or a quarter of an inch, at a time. After each step, allow the subject only one attempt to name the letter. This reduces the subject's chances of guessing the correct letter by a process of elimination. For the same reason, present each letter initially *just* beyond the distance at which, in the pilot trials, the subject could name the letter correctly. You may have to adjust the 'starting point' for letter presentation whilst testing a subject for two possible reasons: first, if your subject gets the letter correct on his first attempt; and second, if your subject does not get the letter correct after nearly ten attempts.

Depending on whether you are using a metre rule or a tape measure, record the threshold distance in centimetres, to the nearest millimetre, or inches to the nearest tenth of an inch. In doing so, remember to allow for the fact that the centre of the rule or measure is *not* at zero. This means that you will have to subtract the numerical value on the tape or measure at the mid-point from the value, either side of the mid-point, at which the subject correctly identifies the letter.

If you are testing 'naïve' subjects – that is, individuals who have not read about the experiment – then you will need to explain the procedure to them so that they are quite clear about what is going to happen and how they are expected to respond in the testing situation. You must also impress upon the subjects the importance of fixating properly during each attempt to read the letter. A few people may find this so difficult as to be almost impossible, and you may have to bring on a substitute subject if this happens. Also, as you will have realized, it is not possible to fixate on one point for very long, and so it is best to allow your subjects to 'rest' between *each* attempt at reading the letter by closing their eyes. After each attempt say 'Eyes closed,' and when you've moved the letter to the next position, say 'Fixate.'

Finally, before testing each subject on the ten 'experimental' letters, run a few pilot trials, as described earlier, using different letters. This is the easiest way to familiarize the subject with the procedure. It also gives the experimenter a check, for each subject, on the best starting point for the initial presentation of each letter.

3.3 Treatment of results

Having completed the running of the experiment, the next step is to fill in the two bottom rows of your scoring sheet (see Table 4). That is, we must determine the total, and then the mean distances, for each subject separately under each condition, at which the ten letters were correctly identified. For each subject tested we will now have two mean distances, one for presentation to the left of the visual field and one for presentation to the right of the visual field. These mean values can be tabulated in a table of results such as the one shown in Table 5 for ten subjects.

There is no point, incidentally, in giving the mean values to more than one decimal place. Though we could give several decimal places, the later figures would be pretty meaningless considering the relative crudeness of our measuring procedure.

Table 5 Mean recognition thresholds for letters presented to the right and to the left of the visual field

	Visual field	
	Left	Right
Subject: 1		
2		
3		
4		
5		
6		
7		
8		
9		
10		
Σ		
x̄		

47

It may be that, merely by inspection (or what in America they call 'the eyeball test'), a clear difference between the two conditions will be apparent. Whether or not this is the case, we will want to summarize the results by obtaining the overall mean scores for the two conditions separately. Having obtained these two mean values, a quick way of testing whether or not the two differ significantly is to do a Sign test. If, say, nine or ten of the ten individual subject means in Table 5 are in the same direction of difference, then there is not very much point in carrying out any further analysis. If we need (or wish) to carry out a more powerful statistical analysis, the related t-test is appropriate (A8, Ch. 5). We suggested the use of these two tests in the previous experiment (see section 2.4). Note that, in choosing this analysis, we have assumed that our scores meet the relevant assumptions underlying the use of the appropriate parametric test.

In evaluating the results of the test, we have to bear in mind that, strictly speaking, our hypothesis implies a one-tailed test. We had predicted that the letters would be recognized more easily when presented to the right of the visual field than when presented to the left. That is, our prediction was that the mean distance of correct letter recognition would be *greater* for presentation to the right of the visual field than to the left.

3.4 Interpretation of results

In section 3.1 we discussed two possible outcomes of this experiment. The purpose of the experiment was to replicate the previous study by Mishkin and Forgays (1952). These authors had found that words were recognized more easily when presented to the right of the visual field than when presented to the left. They suggested that the greater sensitivity to verbal material presented to the right of the visual field was due to changes in our perceptual organisation resulting from learning to read English in the left-to-right direction. This account is in good agreement with theories such as that of Hebb (1949), which stress the importance of the learning component in perceptual organization. The results obtained in our experiment may be similar to those obtained earlier by Mishkin and Forgays, and, if that is so, we could account for our results in a similar way.

We had also suggested, however, that the results obtained

48

by Mishkin and Forgays might have been due to the fact that they presented words, rather than symmetrical capital letters. The point about using words was that the first few letters of a word (which the subject sees first in the right visual field) convey more information about that word than do the last few letters (which the subject sees first in the left visual field). It is easier to guess the correct word given its initial letters than it is given its final letters. Thus, subjects may have recognized words more easily when presented to the right visual field than when presented to the left for this reason alone. If that is so, then the outcome we would expect in our experiment is that there will be no difference between the two conditions, and that the capital letters will be recognized just as easily when presented to the left of the visual field as when presented to the right. If, indeed, our results indicate that this is the case, then two implications emerge. First, such results suggest that the previous results obtained by Mishkin and Forgays were attributable to the artefact associated with their use of words as the presentation material. Second, it would also follow that our results provide no support for the notion that our perceptual organization is modified by our experience of learning to read English in a left-to-right direction.

Finally, we had perhaps better just mention a third possible outcome of the experiment. It is possible that the results indicate that letters are recognized more easily when presented to the *left* of the visual field than when presented to the right. If your results turn out this way, we cannot help you! We can think of no reason to expect such an outcome nor any way of accounting for it theoretically. We would, however, bet that the most likely cause of such a result is what the statistician calls sampling error, due to testing too few subjects.

3.5 Discussion points

This experiment was a replication of a previous study. In section 2.5 we discussed the general value of replicating experiments. One unique experimental result may well give statistical significance in that the probability of that result being due to chance is one in twenty, or less. That it is very unlikely that a particular result is due to chance does not, of course, mean that the result could not be due to chance. Even very rare events do occur sometimes. Thus, our belief in the

49

reliability of a particular experimental result is considerably increased if a number of experimenters, quite independently, replicate the experiment and obtain similar results.

In one sense, replication means exact duplication of the experimental design and procedure. In our experiment here, however, we altered *one* crucial aspect of the previous study's design, in presenting the capital letters as our stimulus material, rather than words. We did this because we suggested that the results of the previous study might have been due to an artefact associated with the use of words as the stimulus material. Since we altered only the one variable (stimulus material) and in all other respects duplicated the procedure of the previous study, then we can argue that any *discrepancy* between the results we obtained, and those obtained in the previous study, are associated with that one variable.

Thus, the logic underlying our replication is essentially the same as the logic underlying our basic experimental design. That is, we attempt to control *all* aspects of the testing situation which are normally free to vary, *except* one, our independent variable, which we deliberately manipulate. In the case of our replication, of course, we attempted to keep all aspects of the testing situation similar to the previous study, except for the one variable (stimulus material) which we changed.

If our experimental results are similar to those obtained in the previous study, then we have, in effect, increased the generality of this particular experimental finding. We will have shown that the result is true for letters, as well as for words. That being the case, then the experimental finding cannot be attributed entirely to the artefact associated with the use of words as the stimulus material.

We have used the word 'artefact' several times in discussing this experiment, and relied on the context to convey its meaning. What we have been demonstrating is how another factor may be confounded with the independent variable. The independent variable here was the side of the visual field at which the stimulus material was presented. The factor confounded with this variable was that the initial letters of a word provide more information about that word than do its last letters. Thus, the experimental results might have been due to this artefact in the sense that we do not know whether the differences obtained in the dependent variable (recognition threshold) were indeed due to this characteristic of words rather than to our manipulation of the independent variable.

In the three experiments we have described, in each case we chose only two conditions: horizontal or vertical orientation of the Müller-Lyer illusion; common or uncommon solution words of anagrams; presentation to the left or to the right of the visual field. While two is the minimum number of conditions required to determine whether or not the independent variable has any effect upon the dependent variable, one may, of course, test more than two conditions. Although one can obtain a great deal of useful information from the simple two-condition experiment, the disadvantage of such designs is that the outcome of the experiment tells one very little about the underlying relationship between the dependent and independent variables.

This point can best be illustrated graphically. Suppose we obtain results such as those shown in Figure 4(a).

The most obvious way to connect our two mean values is by a straight line, as in Figure 4(b). In doing so, however, we are

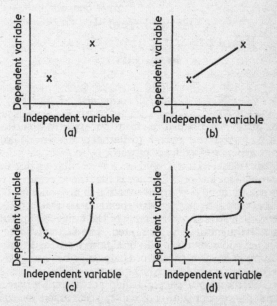

Fig. 4 *Relationship between dependent and independent variables in a two-condition experiment*

assuming a linear, increasing relationship exists between the two variables. As Figure 4(*c*) and 4(*d*) illustrate, other kinds of relationship are possible. Further, on the basis of only two conditions being tested, we have no means of really telling what the relationship between the variables is. That being so, it is difficult to *generalize* from our results. Put another way, on the basis of a difference between our two conditions we can conclude only that variable *A* (the independent variable) has an effect upon variable *B* (the dependent variable). We cannot say anything about what *sort* of effect variable *A* has on variable *B*.

We may, however, sometimes have good grounds on which to predict a particular relationship between two variables. The following experiment is an example of this, and the prediction is that there is a linear trend relationship between the two variables.

Experiment 4
Remembering approximations
to English

4.1 Theoretical background

Approximation to English refers to how closely a particular sequence of words corresponds to normal prose. One could, for example, generate a sequence of words by sampling at random from a dictionary. How would such a word sequence differ from prose? One major difference is that the selection of each successive randomly sampled word imposes no constraint upon the selection of the next word. In normal prose, the choice of one particular word imposes constraints on the choice of the following word. Suppose, for example, we choose the word 'The' and ask you to add one more word, as if starting the beginning of a sentence. Our choice of 'The' has restricted the number of possible words which you could choose: 'Is', 'A' or 'Whether', for example, would not be appropriate. We could further restrict your choice if we again asked you to add one more appropriate word, but this time we choose the first *two* words, for example: 'The boy'. If we begin with three words, such as 'The boy sat', and again asked you to add one more appropriate word, we have by now narrowed down your choice of possible words to a relatively small number. In effect, the more words which we give you as the start of the sentence, the more limited is your choice of the next possible appropriate word.

This characteristic of word sequences can be exploited to generate various 'levels' of approximation to normal prose. Suppose, for example, we take the instance in which two words are given and you are asked to add a third appropriate word. This leads, say, to the phrase 'The boy played'. Suppose you now give the last two words, 'Boy played', to someone else and ask him to add a third appropriate word. This leads, say, to 'The boy played football'. If you now give the last two words 'Played football' to another individual, and continue to repeat this procedure, so that each successive individual is given only the last two words of the sequence, then you may end up with a sequence like 'The boy played football when it came through the window was open at page . . .'

This procedure yields an example of what Miller and Selfridge (1950) called a third order approximation to English. To create a second order approximation, you should start with only one word, and each successive individual who supplied a word should be given only the last word added to the sequence. Similarly, to create a fourth order approximation, you begin with three words, and each successive individual is given the last three words added to the sequence. A fifth order approximation is, not surprisingly, very close to being normal prose.

Miller & Selfridge (1950) investigated the effect of order of approximation to English on subjects' ability to recall word sequences, and our experiment is based on their study. Our prediction is that the higher the order of approximation (that is, the closer the word sequence is to normal prose), the more easily will subjects be able to recall the words. In addition to being intuitively attractive, this prediction is based on the general notion that the closer new material to be learnt is to our previous experience, the more easily we can learn the new material. Since we are used to processing word sequences in terms of meaning, the more meaningful the sequence, the better we shall be able to remember it.

Note that this prediction is different in kind from any we have made in the previous experiments. We are here predicting a relationship between our independent and dependent variables. The relationship we are predicting is that known as a linear trend. That is, we expect that the number of words that subjects will recall from a particular sequence will increase as the order of approximation to English increases.

Our aim is to test the prediction that recall of words from particular word sequences will increase as those sequences approximate closer to normal English prose. Since we are here concerned with a relationship between the two variables, we will need to test more than two conditions. Our first major design decision will be to determine how many conditions to include.

4.2 Method

Design

As we demonstrated in section 3.5, we cannot make any reliable inference concerning the relationship between two variables on the basis of having tested two conditions only. How many conditions do we need to test? While the more conditions we include, the more reliable the information we obtain about the relationship between the two variables, we can in many cases obtain a fairly accurate idea of the relationship on the basis of testing four conditions. We will therefore decide to use four orders of approximation to English. An optimal choice would be to test a zero order of approximation (randomly selected words), a second order of approximation, a fourth order of approximation, and a sequence of normal prose. The word sequences we will use are taken from the Miller and Selfridge study and are given in Appendix II. The subjects for this experiment should not, of course, see these stimulus materials before being tested.

Note that there is a degree of arbitrariness in our choice of the *particular* values of the independent variable which we have decided to use as conditions in the experiment. Often, this kind of decision is made largely on the grounds of just what seems to be intuitively reasonable. A further point worth emphasizing is that, in choosing the particular values of the independent variable to manipulate as conditions in the experiment, we are in effect taking a sample from the whole range of possible values which we could have chosen.

Our next decision is whether to use a between-subjects or

a within-subjects design. We have discussed some of the grounds upon which this decision may be based in the previous experiments. Since, as we have pointed out earlier, the within-subjects design is the more sensitive of the two, and also more 'economical' in terms of the number of subjects we need to test, we will again opt for a within-subjects design in this experiment. An example of a between-subjects experiment where more than two conditions are tested is given in Experiment 7.

So far, then, we have decided on a within-subjects design, and four conditions to be tested. In essence, we will be presenting each subject with four successive lists of words to memorize, and subsequently be asking him to recall as many words as he can from each list. We are expecting that the number of words that the subject can recall will increase as a function of the degree to which the lists approximate to normal prose. We have to consider next what other possible variables might affect subjects' recall performance in this situation, and how to control these other variables.

One variable that is very likely to affect the subjects' recall performance is the length of time we allow the subject to study each list. The longer we allow the subject to learn each list, the better he is likely to be able to remember it. So we will need to ensure that subjects spend the same amount of time in learning the words in each of our four lists. The amount of time we allow will depend on the number of words in each list. Since each list comprises a sequence of fifty words (we also, for similar reasons, have the same number of words in each list), then 2 minutes will be a reasonable amount of time to allow the subject to learn each list. We will need to be fairly precise in our procedure, and give *exactly* 2 minutes study time for each list.

Similar considerations apply to the amount of time we allow the subject for recalling the words in each list. It might seem only fair to allow the subject as much time for recall as he feels he needs. Certainly we should allow sufficient time for recall to allow the subject to recall as many words as he can. But there is a further reason for preferring to standardize recall time, so that the same amount of time is given for recall of each list. This is so that total time interval between the presentation of successive lists remains constant. Three minutes recall time should be sufficient, and we will allow the 3 minutes for each list, whether or not the subject appears to have recalled all the words he can remember before the 3 minutes has elapsed. Thus, allowing 2 minutes for study time, and 3 minutes for recall, we will have a constant 5 minutes interval between the presentation of successive lists.

Having controlled for the effects of possible variables associated with the timing of the testing situation, we should next consider how to control for the effects of possible variables associated with the *order* in which we present the four different list conditions. This, by now, is a familiar design problem, and we advocate here the solution we have proposed in previous experiments – that is, randomizing the order in which we present the four different lists separately for each subject.

Notice that we have implicitly made a further design decision in electing to test each subject only once under each condition. We could have decided to present each subject with several different lists under each condition, several different prose passages, several different sequences of second order approximation, and so on. In the previous experiment, for example, we had ten measures of peripheral recognition to each side of the visual field. In the present experiment, however, we are fairly confident that a single measure of recall from each subject under each condition will be sufficiently reliable.

Finally, we should specify more precisely the nature of our dependent variable in this experiment – that is, recall performance. What we will be scoring is the number of words which subjects recall accurately from each of the four word lists. We could allow the subject to recall orally, or ask him to write down all the words he can recall. Which of these two possibilities we opt for depends, in this case, largely on which is more convenient for the experimenter. If the subject is instructed to recall orally, the experimenter has to record his recall as it occurs. There are several difficulties arising from this procedure, including the fact that the experimenter will have to be monitoring the timing of the test phase at the same time as recording recall performance. From the experimenter's point of view it will be much easier if the subject is instructed to write down the words he can remember at the time of recall.

Procedure
As before, the experiment can be run in a class or group context by selecting, at random, half the group to act as experimenters and the other half as subjects, so that each experimenter tests only one subject. Alternatively, the experiment

can be run on an individual basis with one experimenter testing all the subjects. In either case, we should recommend testing a minimum of ten subjects.

The experimenter should first prepare the word lists (see Appendix II) in a suitable form for presentation to the subject, by transcribing each list separately on to blank cards or paper. In order to randomize the order in which the lists are presented to the subject, they can simply be shuffled prior to testing each subject. The experimenter can also, prior to running the experiment, prepare the data sheet as shown in Table 6 below, although in this case the data will not be scored until after the subjects have been tested.

Table 6 Number of words recalled as a function of order of approximation to English

	Order of approximation			
	O	2	4	Text
Subject: 1				
2				
3				
4				
5				
6				
7				
8				
9				
10				
Σ				
$\bar{x}$				

Either a stop watch or the second hand of an ordinary wrist watch can be used by the experimenter to control the times allowed for study and recall of each list. The subject will need simply four sheets of paper, on which to write down the words he can recall from each list.

If naïve subjects are being tested, they should be fully briefed as to the procedure of the experiment. The subjects should be instructed that they will be shown, in turn, several different lists of words, and that they will be allowed 2 minutes to study each list. At the end of the 2 minute period the experimenter should remove the list and instruct the subject to write down all the words he can remember from that list on the first sheet of paper in front of him. The subjects should be asked to write down the words as accurately as they can, but told that the words do not necessarily have to be in the right order. At the end of the first 3 minute recall period, the experimenter should remove the subject's first recall sheet and at the same time place in front of him the next list of words. This procedure is repeated until all four lists have been presented and recalled, the experimenter being careful to ensure that the time sequence of the presentation and recall periods is adhered to as closely as possible.

4.3 Treatment of results

In our previous experiments the data were scored during the testing of the subjects. Since this was not the case in the present experiment, our first task now is to score the data. For each of the four lists presented to each subject, check the number of words which the subject recalled correctly from the list and enter the total obtained into the Table of Results (see Table 6).

Although this procedure for scoring sounds simple, there are several problems that may arise. First, one may wonder whether or not to score words as correct only if they are recalled in their correct order. Order of recall can be of interest in its own right, but for our purposes we are interested simply in the *number* of words recalled accurately from each list, regardless of order, and so we will not take order of recall into account. Second, each list of words contains several words which are duplicated, particularly words such as 'A', 'The', 'And', etc. Scoring these words may be problematical. One does not always know which particular 'The' the subject has recalled, and he may have recalled more 'The's' than there were in the list. The best solution is probably to allow as correct each of such words which he recalls up to the total number that were in the list. Lastly, the subjects may sometimes have recalled words which, though not absolutely correct, are very similar to words in the original list. Here one could be either 'charitable' or 'uncharitable' in deciding whether or not to accept such words as being correct. Probably it is simpler to be uncharitable, and to accept as correct only those words which are recalled in exactly the same form as they appeared on the original list. By doing so, it is easier to make sure that one's scoring criterion is consistent across lists and subjects. One might, however, exempt obvious spelling errors from this rule. The important point to remember in considering criteria for scoring data such as these is that one's scoring procedure must be clearly consistent for all lists and all subjects.

Having scored the data and completed the table of results, the mean number of words recalled under each of the four conditions should be calculated. These mean values can then be plotted on a graph, so that we can see at a glance whether or not the results more or less conform with our expectations. We had predicted a linear increase in recall scores as a function of the degree of approximation to English of each of the four lists, with the zero order of approximation giving the lowest recall scores, and normal prose giving the highest. The appropriate statistical analysis given by Miller is Page's L-test, rather than Jonckheere's trend test, since we have used a within-subjects design and our data therefore comprise related rather than independent scores. The significance of the trend in our data should therefore be calculated by applying the Page L-test (A8, Chapter 6). Note that our trend prediction involves a one-tailed rather than a two-tailed statistical test, by definition. This is because, in predicting a trend, one is predicting not merely that there will be differences between the conditions, but one is also predicting the direction of the differences. In this case, we predicted that the measures on our dependent variable (recall scores) would *increase* as the value along our independent variable (order of approximation) increased. One final point to be noted in passing is that the Page L-test is a non-parametric trend test, and our data may well be appropriately analysed by means of parametric tests. Our choice of the non-parametric trend test is largely because the equivalent parametric form of analysis is beyond the scope of most introductory statistics texts.

4.4 Interpretation of results

Assuming that we have obtained a statistically significant result from our trend analysis, then we may conclude that subjects' recall performance does indeed improve as the order of approximation to English of the word sequences increases. This does not imply, however, that particular *pairs* of the conditions we tested differ significantly from each other. Inspection of the graph of our results may indicate, for instance, that whereas the difference between the zero order and the second order conditions is fairly large, the difference between the fourth order and normal prose is relatively small. We may wish to know exactly which pairs of conditions differ significantly from each other. To determine this, we could further analyse the data across various pairs of conditions using the appropriate two-condition test. While such further analysis would yield more information about the pattern of differences in the data than does the trend test alone, there are risks involved. With four conditions in all, the total number of pair-wise comparisons we could make between conditions is six. The more such tests we carry out, the more likely we are to conclude that there is a significant difference between a pair of conditions when, in fact, there is not. Suppose, for example, one did a hundred such tests. Five out of the hundred would yield a 'significant' result at $p < 0.05$ and one out of a hundred would yield a 'significant' result at $p < 0.01$, but in both cases these 'significant' results would be due to chance. We discussed a rather similar point in section 2.5. In effect, a statistically significant result means only that the observed event could only rarely occur by chance. The more statistical tests we carry out on the same set of data, the more likely it is that we will 'obtain' a rare event which is, in fact, due to chance. Hence, while further tests on the data can be carried out, we should be very cautious in interpreting the outcomes of such tests. One possibility, for example, would be to raise our criterion from $p < 0.05$ to $p < 0.01$ before accepting that a 'real' difference exists between pairs of conditions.

Leaving aside the possibilities (and hazards) of further analysis of the data, let us turn now to a more theoretical level of interpretation. The results of this experiment will have shown that recall improves as order of approximation to English increases. We can describe this outcome in terms of the effects of context upon ease of learning: the more familiar the context, the easier it is to learn the 'novel' material. Put another way, we could think of learning as involving the integration of relatively novel material into the relatively permanent body of knowledge which we have acquired through past experience. The results of the present experiment suggest that the more 'familiar' the novel material, the more easily we can assimilate it.

We could take our understanding of the results of the present experiment a step further if we examine the data in terms of what Tulving and Patkau (1962) called 'adopted chunks'. An adopted chunk is defined, operationally, as any sequence of words, or single word, which the subject recalls accurately from the original list. For instance, given the original example, 'The boy played football when it came through the window was open at page', suppose the subject wrote down at recall: 'Page, the boy played football, it came through the window'. Scored in terms of adopted chunks, there are three chunks in these recall data. An adopted chunk is any sequence of words in recall, regardless of length, which corresponds with the original list.

If you re-score the recall data in terms of adopted chunks, you should find that the number of chunks is more or less the same regardless of the order of approximation to English. That is, the subjects tend to recall the same number of chunks in each of the four conditions, but while the number of chunks remains constant, the *size* of the chunks increases as the original list approximates more closely to English (i.e. subjects recall more words per chunk).

What does this result suggest? First, it shows that our independent variable (approximation to English) has an effect only upon the number of words per chunk and does not affect the actual number of chunks. This suggests that the subject's recall performance reflects *two* independent *processes*: one to do with the *number* of chunks, and one to do with the *size* of the chunks. Since the number of chunks remains constant, it seems as though the number of chunks which subjects can recall reflects a basic limitation in our information processing capacity. One way of overcoming this limitation is to increase the amount of information contained in each chunk. The amount of information contained in each chunk can be increased more easily when that information corresponds more closely to our past experience and previous learning.

4.5 Discussion points

In this experiment we selected four values of our independent variable. In section 3.5, we pointed out that if only two values were tested, the relationship between the independent and dependent variables remained unclear. To determine the relationship between two variables one has to test more than two values of the independent variable. The present experiment involved the prediction of a particular relationship – that of linear trend.

The experimenter is almost always, of course, interested in more than the particular values of the independent variable which he chooses to test. He may wish to generalize his results from the particular values tested to other untested values. For example, consider some fictional data illustrated in Figure 5.

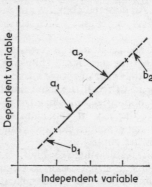

Fig. 5 *Generalizing from selected values of the independent variable*

The relationship depicted is that of a linear trend. Three values of the independent variable are shown. One assumes continuity in the relationship shown, such that both points representing intermediate values of the independent variable (a_1 and a_2) and values which lie outside the range of those tested (b_1 and b_2) will conform with the actual values sampled in the experiment. In effect, one is using the results obtained in the particular experiment to predict the results of other experiments not carried out.

It is obvious that one's choice of appropriate values of the independent variable is as critical a feature of the experiment as is one's use of an appropriate design, proper sampling of subjects, and so on. And although the risk of error is greatest when attempting to generalize from only two values of the independent variable, the same kind of risk is inherent in generalizing from more than two values. In general, the more widely the values sampled reflect the whole range of possible values, the less the risk involved. Note, however, that these considerations depend also on the nature of the independent variable. In the peripheral recognition experiment, for example, there were only two possible values of our independent variable – the right and the left side of the visual field respectively.

There are no 'hard and fast' rules governing one's choice of appropriate values of the independent variable. Often this decision is governed largely by the results of similar previous experiments and the current state of knowledge in the field. Our choice of zero, second, fourth orders of approximation and normal prose as the conditions in the present experiment was based partly on the intuitive feeling that these values seem fairly evenly spaced, and partly on our desire to demonstrate a linear trend relationship. And herein lies another 'moral'. One source of experimental bias which we have not yet mentioned is that the expectations of the experimenter may themselves influence the outcome of the experiment. Experimenter bias may operate at several levels. For example, the expectations of the experimenter will influence the decisions he makes about the particular values of the independent variable to test, the appropriate dependent variable, and so on. Also, in the test phase of the experiment, the experimenter may, perhaps unwittingly, react in a different way to subjects in an experimental group than he does to subjects in a control group. Or, in a within-subjects design, he may again perhaps unwittingly reinforce subjects when their performance appears to be conforming to his expectations. The effects of experimenter bias have been well documented by Rosenthal (1963).

Finally, you may well by now have concluded that it seems impossible to control fully for the effects of all the possible variables which could bias the outcome of any particular experiment. This is so. By and large, in designing an experiment one focuses on the control of the likely *relevant* variables. In the present experiment you may recall that we used only one list of words for each of our four conditions and that each list comprised different words. Thus we assumed that the actual nature of the words themselves was not likely to be a relevant variable. The 'cost' of this decision is that one could argue that the results of our experiment were attributable to, say, the relative difficulty of learning the particular words in each list rather than to their order of approximation to English. This possible source of bias could have been eliminated only by using exactly the same words in each of the four lists. However, the way in which the lists were constructed precludes us from having exactly the same words in each list. We could, though, have reduced the possible effects of this source of bias by using a number of different lists in each condition. In effect, this procedure would increase the number of different words sampled in each condition and thereby increase the likelihood that our results will be true for the population of words in general.

Experiment 5
Expectancy in the perception
of ambiguous stimuli

5.1 Theoretical background

Under the influence of the German Gestalt school of psychology in the first half of this century, perception was considered to be a passive process, involving fairly exact registration of the stimulus, analogous to a photographic imprint. The coming of the 1940s saw a rebellion against this view. The 'New look' in perception, led by Bruner and Postman in America, envisaged perception not as a passive receptor system, but as a dynamic process of information analysis. Recognition was given to the fact that perception involves not only *reception* but also *interpretation* of stimulus information, so that it becomes meaningful to the observer, and therefore that sensory stimulus characteristics are not the sole determinants of perception; other factors, arising within the observer, have an active role to play.

One of these factors is a cognitive one – that of expectancy, preparedness, or set. For example, the stimulus pattern in Figure 6 may be perceived in at least two ways – as a rabbit or a pelican. Which of these is initially perceived will be influenced by the expectancy of the observer. If he has been told that this is an animal with long ears, the 'rabbit' interpretation is the more probable one. The effects of set, in general, are that what is more familiar, more probable and expected, is perceived more readily than, or to the exclusion of, that which is less familiar and unexpected.

Fig. 6 *The rabbit-pelican interchangeable figure*

Research has shown that the origin of set lies in the past experience of the individual. This may be relatively short term, arising, for example, from instructions given immediately prior to perception – e.g. that Figure 6 represents a long-eared animal. Set induced in this way is explicit, in that the perceiver is aware of it. Alternatively, set may be built up over a long period of time. The experience of everyday life leads to the formation of expectancies about relationships between certain objects, characteristics, and events: that grass is green, that the letter Q is followed by U, etc. These types of expectancies, which the individual brings with him to an experimental situation, provide *implicit* sets, in that the individual is not *consciously* aware of them at the time of the experiment.

The conditions under which the operation of set can most readily be demonstrated in a laboratory setting are those where the stimulus situation is ambiguous, for it is in this situation that the determining role of stimulus characteristics is minimized, while that of the individual's cognitive set is maximized. Stimulus ambiguity may be achieved by the use of supra-threshold stimuli (i.e. stimuli exposed with sufficient intensity and duration for sensory characteristics to be clearly registered) which have more than one possible meaning e.g. the rabbit-pelican figure. Another way of introducing ambiguity is the use of stimuli which are just at, or just above, the threshold of clear perception (this can be achieved by using very brief exposures, or very low stimulus intensity).

The effects of set on perception are varied, and can be measured in a number of ways, but the two most commonly used measures are the nature of the qualitative response interpretation given to the stimulus (how the stimulus is described), and the speed with which the stimulus is perceived. An experiment by Duncker (1939) illustrates the former measure. He showed that the *perceived* colour of identically coloured flat grey shapes was influenced by their outline: leaf shapes were perceived as greener, banana shapes as more yellow. The inference is that the past experience of the subjects with leaves and bananas has induced an implicit set about colour-shape relations, and led to differential perception of the same physical stimulus.

A classical study by Howes and Solomon (1951) provides an example of speed of recognition as a measure of the effect of set. Recognition thresholds of words of comparable length but varying frequency of occurrence in the language, and hence varying degrees of familiarity, were measured. It was found that words which have a higher probability of occurrence had lower thresholds of recognition (i.e. needed a shorter exposure duration) than less familiar words. It seemed that the subjects had, on the basis of their knowledge of the language, an implicit set for words which tend to occur more frequently, and were therefore 'tuned' to perceive them.

However, these and similar experimental findings were soon the centre of controversy. The problem, one of considerable theoretical importance, was whether the effect of set was to influence *perceptual* processing, or whether it affected response selection, narrowing the alternatives from which the subject is likely to choose a response. Since the stimulus situation is always in some way ambiguous, to some extent a subject is guessing at what the stimulus represents. For example, in the Howes and Solomon study, it could be argued that lower thresholds were obtained for familiar words not because the perceptual process was more attuned to deal with them, but because they were readily available in the subject's *response* repertoire and were therefore produced as 'guesses'.

Many apparent demonstrations of the role of set in perception could be accounted for by the 'response interpretation' of the effects of set, a more prosaic hypothesis. There are, however, some findings for which it would be extremely difficult to provide a response-interpretation, and which militate for the 'perceptual tuning' hypothesis of the effects of set. Bruner and Postman (1949) investigated recognition thresholds for playing cards, some of which had incongruous combinations of colour and suit, e.g. black diamonds, red spades. On the basis of past experience with playing cards, subjects would have an implicit set for 'normal' colour-suit combinations – e.g. red hearts, etc. Recognition thresholds for 'incongruous' cards were much higher than those for 'normal' cards; this is open to the criticism that it demonstrates the influence of set not on perception, but on guessing habits, since no one is likely to attempt to guess at 'red spades', for example. Evidence that perceptual processing *was* affected by set came from some of the pre-recognition guesses made by subjects, e.g. 'a purple card', 'rusty coloured', 'black with red edges'. Responses such as these could not have been prompted by the subject's past experience with playing cards; they suggest that the processes of perceptual analysis have been affected in a bizarre manner by the conflict between expectation and actual sensory information. However, the fact that set has been shown to affect perception in some cases does not free other research in the area from the response interpretation of set effects, and all findings should be evaluated and interpreted individually and with caution.

The present experiment has been devised to examine the effects of set in a simple situation involving the perception of ambiguous words.

The words may be interpreted either as the names of animals, or as words unrelated to animals, and the set-inducing procedure aims to tune the perceptual process to the perception of animal names. The set is induced implicitly during the experiment; the use of implicit set, avoiding subjects' awareness of it, eliminates the possibility of the results being confounded by subjects responding in accordance with, or possibly against, what they perceive as the required type of response.

The general prediction which can be made in the light of past research is that the effect of set will be to increase the incidence of perception of animal names.

5.2 Method

Design

The experimental design involves two conditions; in one, the *experimental* condition, set will be induced in the subjects, and their performance on the perceptual task, the perception of ambiguous words, will be tested. The other condition is a *control* condition, in which performance on the perceptual task is tested *without* any set being induced; this will provide a base level measure of what performance is like under 'ordinary' conditions on that particular perceptual task. The difference between the Experimental and Control condition data will indicate the extent to which set induction affected perceptual processes.

Each subject can only be tested under one of the conditions; repetition of the perceptual test on the same subject would render the experiment devoid of meaning. Therefore, the two conditions, experimental and control, must be *independent*, or *unrelated*, a different group of subjects being tested under each condition.

The *independent variable* is set induction; it is either induced, or not, which gives rise to the two conditions. The *dependent variable* is the measure of performance on the perceptual task, the extent to which set-related perception occurs. The experimental hypothesis is that there will be a difference between the two conditions, performance in the experimental condition being affected by set. These three concepts are elaborated at the end of the method section.

The experiment falls conceptually into two consecutive phases, one involving set induction, the other, perceptual testing.

Phase 1: Set induction
(i) The experimental design demands that, prior to performance of the perceptual task involving ambiguous words, a set to perceive the names of animals be induced in subjects in the experimental condition. This can be achieved by showing a list of animal names (other than those which may be used as part of the ambiguous test stimuli in phase 2), in such a way that each word is clearly perceived by the subject. This is an example of implicit, short-term induction of set; there is, of course, no guarantee that the procedure is effective in inducing set, though the assumption is justified on the evidence of several similar earlier studies. The list to be used in this set-induction procedure consists of five animal names, and is shown in Table 8.

(ii) In order that the treatment of subjects is comparable under experimental and control conditions, apart from the basic difference in the independent variable – the induction of set – it is essential that subjects in the control condition are also subjected to a procedure of similar nature and duration to the set-induction procedure for experimental subjects. Therefore, control subjects will also be asked to identify a list of words, prior to phase 2 of the experiment. To ensure maximum comparability between these tasks for experimental and control subjects, the lists are matched as far as possible for list length, and length and familiarity of words, though the control list contains no set-related words. The list for use for control subjects is also shown in Table 8.

(iii) In order to disguise the purpose of this phase of the experiment – and this is particularly important for experimental subjects – the phase can be used as an exercise to find the subjects' recognition threshold of perception – that is, the level at which a stimulus can just be perceived and identified. Threshold measures are required for phase 2 of the experiment, when the ambiguous stimulus words will be shown at recognition threshold levels, to ensure favourable conditions for the operation of set.

(iv) Achievement of threshold levels. An efficient way of reducing physical stimulus intensity to such a level that it falls to below a threshold level is to use a tachistoscope for stimulus presentation (see section on equipment and materials). A tachistoscope permits controlled variation, down to very low levels, of exposure duration or intensity of a stimulus. Use variation in *exposure duration* to produce changes in the physical value of the stimulus; your measures of stimulus values will be expressed in terms of milliseconds. If you do not have access to a tachistoscope you can degrade the physical quality and intensity of a stimulus by placing it under layers of tissue paper.

(v) Determination of thresholds. The threshold must be determined *individually* for each subject, as there are considerable individual differences in thresholds – a stimulus which falls well below the threshold of one subject may be clearly perceptible to another.

Theoretically a recognition threshold is the level of physical stimulus intensity at which the stimulus can be recognized 50 per cent of the time. In practice, in this experiment, the threshold will be taken as the point at which the subject begins to perceive and identify a stimulus word. There are various methods by which the threshold can be determined accurately, but in this experiment it will suffice to use the following adaptation. Begin with the stimulus intensity well below the

69

threshold, so that the subject can perceive nothing; that is, set the tachistoscope on a very brief exposure time, or use a large number of layers of tissue paper. Gradually increase the stimulus duration by small grades, testing at each stage whether the subject can identify the stimulus. If using tissue paper, increase the stimulus intensity by removing one layer of paper at each trial. The level just below that at which the subject succeeds in identifying the stimulus is the threshold measure for that stimulus.

(vi) This threshold determination procedure will be carried out on each of the five words to be presented to the subject during phase 1. As a final measure of each subject's threshold take the *mean* value of the threshold readings for the five words, and use this as the level at which, or just below which, ambiguous test stimuli are presented in phase 2. At this level the stimuli should be sufficiently degraded to preclude clear perception, yet carry sufficient information for some perceptual processing to occur, thereby creating conditions under which set may play a determining role.

(vii) Since the purpose of phase 1 requires that the set-inducing and control words should be clearly perceived by the subjects, the presentation of each word should continue after correct identification, to a level well *above* the threshold. The same level, e.g. two exposures after correct identification, should be reached for all words and all subjects.

Phase 2: Perception of ambiguous words

(i) The perceptual task. A list of ambiguous stimulus words is presented, presentation being visual and consecutive, and the subject's task is to identify each word. Ambiguity of the stimuli is derived from each word being composed of two superimposed words; one of these is an animal name, the other – a control word – unrelated to the set concept, but matched as far as possible with the animal name in terms of other variables which could affect perception: length, visual form and frequency of occurrence in the language (familiarity). For example, the two words, set and control, may be:

DOG and DIG

which, superimposed, form the ambiguous stimulus:

DØG

and this may be perceived as either of the two constituent

words. To introduce further ambiguity into the stimulus situation, thereby ensuring that subjects do not perceive the structure of the stimulus words, the stimuli are presented under conditions of reduced physical intensity – specifically, just below recognition threshold level.

Ten ambiguous test stimuli have been prepared, and are shown in Table 9.

(ii) Measure of performance. The critical aspect of performance on this task is perceptual interpretation of each ambiguous stimulus – as the set-related animal name, or as the control word. The data required for analysis will be the *number* of set-related perceptions. The performance of subjects in the control condition will provide a base measure of how the test stimuli are interpreted under normal conditions, without set being induced. The performance of subjects in the experimental condition will indicate whether, and to what extent, the set-induction procedure of phase 1 has been effective in determining the perceptual interpretation placed upon the ambiguous stimuli.

In summary, the *independent variable* is the level of set induced – zero in the control condition, some positive but unquantified level in the experimental condition. Set is induced in the experimental subjects during the presentation of a sequence of set-related words.

The *dependent variable* is the number of set-related perceptions from the ambiguous stimuli.

On the basis of past research, the experimental prediction or hypothesis of this experiment is that more set-related perceptual interpretations will occur in the experimental condition than in the control condition.

The overall plan of the experiment is summarized in Table 7.

Materials and Equipment

(i) *The tachistoscope*. This is an instrument which has facilities for controlling the duration of exposure (and sometimes the illumination) of a visual stimulus. The basic structure, shown in Figure 7, consists of two compartments divided at an angle of 45° by a semi-silvered mirror.

The visual stimulus, depicted on a white card, is inserted into the slot provided, and falls in the stimulus field. If compartment A is lit up, and B is dim, the subject – looking through the visor – sees the adaptation field, usually a blank

Table 7 Overall plan of the experiment

	Experimental condition (Set induced)	*Control condition* (No set)
Phase 1	Set induction – threshold determination. Five set-related words presented to and identified by subject.	Threshold determination. Five control words, matched with set-induction words, presented to and identified by subject.
Phase 2	Ten ambiguous test words presented at threshold. Subject indicates perception.	Ten ambiguous test words presented at threshold. Subject indicates perception.
Data	Number of set-related perceptual interpretations of ambiguous test words, per subject	Number of set-related perceptual interpretation of ambiguous test words, per subject.

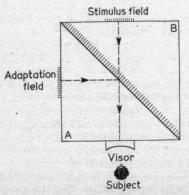

Fig. 7 *Basic structure of a 2-field tachistoscope*

white field with a cross in the centre on which to focus the eyes, which appears directly ahead, but is in fact reflected from the left. Exposure of the stimulus field is effected by depressing a push-button, which extinguishes compartment A and simultaneously lights up compartment B. The subject now sees the stimulus, apparently in the same position, directly ahead, as the adaptation field. The duration of the stimulus exposure is predetermined by the setting of a time selector switch, giving a typical timing range of 1 millisecond to 2 seconds. After the expiry of this time, the fields automatically revert to the adaptation phase.

(ii) *Preparation of stimulus words for presentation.* The lists of words for use in the experimental phases are shown in Tables 8 and 9.

Table 8 Words for use during phase 1 of the experiment

Experimental condition Set-inducing words	Control condition Control words
DOG	DRY
CAT	CELL
HORSE	HOPE
CHICKEN	CENTRAL
TIGER	TEMPER

These sets of words are equated as far as possible for visual form, length and familiarity.

When constructing the stimuli for presentation, *print* each word in the centre of a plain card. Try not to make the superimposed letters in the test stimuli stand out more than the single letters for this may attract the subject's attention, to the detraction of an overall perceptual analysis of the stimulus.

Make sure that you use the *same* test stimulus cards in both experimental and control conditions. This will ensure that any bias towards a particular interpretation of a stimulus, caused by inaccurate stimulus preparation, will be distributed equally across the conditions. To use an extreme example, avoid writing GOAT for use in the experimental condition and GOAT for the control condition.

Table 9 Set-related and control words for use in the construction of ambiguous test stimuli

Set-related words	Ambiguous test stimuli	Control words
1 GOAT	GOAT	GOAL
2 MOUSE	MOUSE	HOUSE
3 SHEEP	SHEEP	STEEP
4 PARROT	PARROT	CARROT
5 HARE	HARD	HARD
6 STOAT	STOAT	STOUT
7 SEAL	PEAL	PEAL
8 DEER	DEER	PEER
9 WHALE	WHOLE	WHOLE
10 WASP	WASP	WISP

Procedure

Allocate your subjects to the conditions on a random basis. The number of subjects in each condition does not have to be equal, but there should be a minimum of eight, preferably ten, subjects per condition. Having assigned a subject to one of the conditions, describe what he is required to do, without divulging anything about the purpose of the experiment. For example, present the experiment as having 'something to do with perception'. Allow the subject a few practice trials, using stimuli extraneous to the experiment proper, to accustom him to the procedure. This is particularly important if you are using a tachistoscope.

Each trial during phase 1 of the experiment will involve the following sequence: starting with the stimulus well below threshold level (which you will have estimated approximately from the practice trials), present the stimulus, preceding it by a verbal warning for the subject to be prepared. The subject attempts to identify the stimulus after each presentation. Increase the intensity or exposure duration after each failure of identification, until the subject finally succeeds in identifying the stimulus. Expose the stimulus at least once more, well above threshold level, to ensure that the subject has seen it clearly. You can justify this additional presentation by asking the subject if he is sure about his response, and allowing him to 'try again'. Record the threshold reading – in milliseconds, brightness value or number of layers of tissue paper.

The trials during phase 2 may appear rather similar in procedure, to the subject, to those of phase 1, but there are important differences between them. There is no repeated stimulus presentation beginning with levels far below the threshold, because this could yield too much information to the subject due to summation of information from repeated presentations, even though they are sub-threshold. The level at which the test stimuli are presented is based on the mean of the five threshold values obtained during phase 1 (see phase 1, section (iv)). Ideally, each test stimulus should be exposed only once. The stimuli cannot be clearly exposed to the subject, and problems may arise if a subject requests further exposures during this phase, because he is unsure about the identity of the stimulus and is unprepared to guess. Try to encourage your subject to guess and reassure him that you are interested in the *impression* he obtains, and not in *correct* responses.

Record your subjects' response during phase 2. At the end of the experiment, experimental ethic demands that you explain the true nature of the experiment to your subject, particularly if your instructions led him astray in this respect; but ask the subject not to disclose this information to other potential subjects.

5.3 Treatment of results

From the records of the subjects' responses, obtain a score for each subject, representing the number of set-related (animal) perceptual interpretations of the ambiguous test stimuli produced during phase 2. The maximum score is 10.

Your table of data should appear similar to Table 10.

In order to test whether there is a significant difference between the conditions in the number of set-related perceptions, the data of Table 10 may be analysed by the Mann-Whitney U-test (A8, Chapter 4). This is appropriate because the data are non-parametric (not normally distributed), the scores are discontinuous taking discrete values from 0 to 10, and the two conditions are independent. The test should be a one-tailed test, since a *directional* difference was predicted by the experimental hypothesis – that the mean score in the experimental condition would be higher than in the control condition.

Table 10 Number of set-related perceptions of ambiguous stimuli

	Experimental condition	Control condition
Subjects (S):		
	S_1	S_{11}
	S_2	S_{12}
	S_3	S_{13}
	S_4	S_{14}
	S_5	S_{15}
	S_6	S_{16}
	S_7	S_{17}
	S_8	S_{18}
	S_9	S_{19}
	S_{10}	S_{20}
	$\bar{X}$	$\bar{X}$

5.4 Interpretation of results

Assuming that the stimuli were not biased in a particular direction, and that subjects did not have an inherent set to perceive animal names, the mean score in the control condition should be about 5, i.e. 50 per cent of the total. If this score is much higher, it does suggest that either or both of the assumptions is invalid.

The difference between the means of the scores for the two conditions provides an immediate appreciation of whether set has had an effect in the predicted direction; if it has, then there should be more set-related perceptions in the experimental condition. If the difference is significant on the basis of the statistical analysis, then the data support the experimental hypothesis.

5.5 Discussion points

Several explanations can be offered for any failure of the results to support the experimental hypothesis. One is simply that the set-induction procedure during phase 1 was ineffective in inducing set; such an explanation should be accompanied by suggestions for improved set-induction methods. Another possibility is that the set-induction procedure *was* effective, but that the same set was aroused in control subjects. This could have occurred, not in phase 1, but during the early stages of phase 2, if the first few test stimuli happened to be identified as animal names. In consequence, the condition would cease to be a true control condition, and would be transformed into a 'set' condition, with an uncontrolled extent of set. The number of set-related responses would be spuriously high, and this would decrease the true difference between experimental and control conditions, leading to a failure to achieve significance at the stage of statistical analysis.

One point of interest is that this experiment uses a rather gross measure of performance – number of set-related responses – in place of the more common recognition threshold. It is possible to adapt the procedure of this experiment so that the recognition threshold does become the measure of performance. For example, after set arousal in phase 1, unambiguous animal names could be used as test stimuli in both experimental and control conditions, and recognition threshold measures obtained for all subjects. Lower thresholds (quicker recognition) would be expected in the experimental condition. One of the problems with using such a method, however, is the possibility of set being aroused in control subjects after the first few stimuli had been recognized, a point discussed in the preceding paragraphs. A possible solution to this would be the use of one trial per subject, which would be expensive in terms of subjects.

In view of the controversy over the site of the action of set effects, the only immediate conclusion which can be drawn from results which are statistically significant is that set induction has increased the number of set-related responses. The results do not point unambiguously to perceptual processing being affected by set; they could be consistent with a response interpretation of set effects. For example, it could be that the effect of seeing animal names during phase 1 was to sensitize all conceptually related words in the subject's memory store, so that they became more available as responses, and were produced during phase 2 in preference to other words, on the basis of relatively little sensory information. Therefore, before firm conclusions can be drawn, the experiment needs to be considered very carefully and searched for any features which can serve as a basis of discrimination between perceptual and response interpretations of the effects of set.

Experiment 6
Hand and foot reaction time

6.1 Theoretical background

Reaction time (RT) may be defined as the interval of time between the onset of a stimulus and the onset of a response to that stimulus. The sequence of events involved is shown in Figure 8.

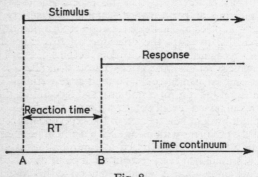

Fig. 8

The time interval between A, the onset of the stimulus, and B, the point at which the response commences, is the reaction time. Contrary to a popular misconception, reaction time is the time needed to *start*, not to complete a response.

When there is only one possible stimulus which can occur, with one predefined response to be made to it, and the only uncertainty about the situation is temporal uncertainty as to when the stimulus will occur, the situation is known as *simple reaction time*. For example, the stimulus may be a red light, and the required response depression of a Morse key with the right hand. When the situation involves two or more stimulus alternatives, each with its associated response, the reaction time is known as either disjunctive, complex or choice RT. For example, the stimulus alternatives may be red and green lights, requiring right and left hand responses respectively. Figure 9 illustrates the differences between simple and complex RT, including examples of variations in complex RT.

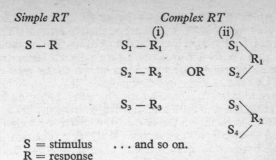

S = stimulus ... and so on.
R = response

Fig. 9 *Simple and complex RT situations*

The chain of processes involved in reaction time, even in the simple situation, is quite complex. The stimulus information impinging on a sense organ in the form of physical energy is transduced into neural impulses, transmitted to the brain, analysed, the response is programmed, and the information necessary for response execution is relayed to the appropriate group of effector muscles. All this takes place within approximately 250 milliseconds ($\frac{1}{4}$ second). Complex RT, involving the additional complications of discrimination between stimuli, and of selection of the appropriate response, is considerably longer.

The study of reaction time has its historical roots in two branches of science – astronomy and physiology. The origin in astronomy can be traced to an incident at the Greenwich observatory in 1795, an incident which began to dispel a prevalent conviction – that response latency was zero. The Astronomer Royal, Maskelyne, noticed that the times recorded by his assistant for the exact moment when a particular stellar constellation was reached were slower than his own, and dismissed the assistant for lack of diligence. That this was a miscarriage of justice became apparent when other discrepancies between individual astronomers' timings were subsequently noted, and it was realized that the discrepancies were due to differences in the speed of responding to a signal, characteristic of each individual. The recognition that speed of responding is not infinite provided the conceptual definition of reaction time.

The role of physiology in the development of reaction time studies can be traced to the pioneering work of the Austrian physiologist Helmholtz, on the conduction of nerve impulses. In the 1850s Helmholtz succeeded in measuring the speed of conduction of nerve impulses by electrically stimulating a motor nerve in a nerve-muscle preparation of a frog at different distances from the muscle, and recording the variation in latency of the 'twitch' reaction in the muscle. The value he obtained for speed of nerve conduction was of the order of 80 metres/second. Using an adaptation of this method he attempted to measure human reaction by electrically stimulating a point on the skin at different distances from the brain, and recording latencies of reaction to the shock. Although this proved unsatisfactory as a method of RT determination, since neural conduction occupies but a small portion of total reaction time, it instigated further investigations into reaction time. The invention of the Hipp chronoscope, an instrument capable of measuring time in units of 1 millisecond (one thousandth of a second), completed the stimulus to a rapid expansion of research in the field of reaction time which has continued for over a century.

This research has resulted in the accumulation of a considerable store of information about reaction time and factors affecting it. For example, simple RT has been shown to be of the order of 180–250 milliseconds, the value depending on the stimulus modality. RTs to auditory stimuli are shorter than those to visual ones. Lack of motivation on the part of the subject increases reaction time, while practice, and feedback about performance on the task, tend to decrease it. Reaction time increases with age, the fastest RTs occurring in the teens.

Chemical substances which affect the nervous system also affect reaction time. For example, depressants, such as alcohol and the barbiturate drugs, produce an increase in RT, while stimulants, such as caffeine and amphetamine drugs, decrease RT.

The study of reaction time has numerous practical applications. It may serve as an indicator of the degree of mastery of a skill, RTs decreasing with an increase in the degree of learning. RT may be used in psycho-analytic word-association tests, where a long RT in response to a stimulus word may be indicative of an area of internal conflict. Considerations of RT are important in ergonomics (man-machine interactions), both in the design of equipment and in analysis of the efficiency of the human operator.

An example drawn from everyday life of this last point is the case of driving a car, a perceptual-motor skill in which it is frequently essential to react with the minimum delay. In fact, driving may be analysed in terms of a series of reaction times, interspersed with motor movements. The reactions are predominantly of the complex type, since there are countless stimulus alternatives, many of which are not precisely defined prior to their occurrence, and which require a variety of responses. For example, a cat may run across the road, requiring a braking response; an overtaking vehicle cuts in too sharply, requiring a steering change; a train looms up while traversing a level crossing, requiring instant acceleration. One of the few situations during driving which involves a simple RT is waiting for red traffic lights to change to green. The stimulus (defined, except for temporal uncertainty) is the green light, and the response is depression of the accelerator, or perhaps a composite response of accelerator depression, release of clutch pedal, and release of hand brake.

An interesting speculation related to the role of reaction time in driving, where both hand and foot limbs are involved in making motor responses, is whether hand reactions yield faster RTs than foot reactions. This seems a plausible hypothesis on the basis of speed of neural conduction, for hand-brain distance is shorter than foot-brain distance. If the hypothesis were to find support in experimental evidence, it could have important implications for the design of equipment involved in a man-machine interface, such as the motor car or aeroplane. Appropriate structure and design could contribute not only to the efficiency but also to the safety of operations. For example, a reduction of even 20 milliseconds in RT could mean a reduction of 90 feet in braking distance when travelling at 60 miles per hour.

The aim of the present experiment is to examine the differences between hand and foot reaction time using a simple RT situation. Although this is not directly comparable with the complex RTs involved in driving a car or piloting an aeroplane, simple RT provides a sound basis of generalization to the more complex reaction time situation. The specific hypothesis which the experiment can test is that hand RTs are faster than foot RTs.

6.2 Method

Design
A comparison between the reaction times of hand reactions and those of foot reactions is required. Therefore, the experimental design is based on two experimental conditions: C_1, in

which simple RT is tested using hand reactions; and C_2, in which simple RT is tested using foot reactions. These conditions will be *independent* or *unrelated*, in that one group of subjects is tested in C_1, another group of subjects in C_2; thus the hand and foot RT scores will arise from *different* subjects. Although it may seem simpler to test the hand and foot RT of the same subject, the use of independent groups avoids certain problems, such as those of order of conducting the tests (see section 2.2). The use of an independent group design does, however, create additional variance in the data due to individual differences in basic RT, regardless of differences due to the use of different limbs when responding. In order to obtain reasonable reliability of data, each subject's RT must be tested more than once; a single RT trial may produce an unrepresentative result, due, for example, to some momentary state of inattention on the part of the subject. Ten test trials per subject should be an adequate minimum, the mean of those ten trials constituting the RT score for each subject.

About eight subjects should be tested in each condition, since the chances of obtaining statistically significant data with fewer than this are low. It is not essential that the number of subjects in each condition be equal, but it does simplify analysis of the data.

The *independent variable* in this experiment is the nature of the response – executed with the hand or the foot. The *dependent variable*, the measure of the subject's performance, is reaction time. At the end of the experiment you should have two sets of scores, one from hand reactions in C_1, the other from foot reactions in C_2, each score representing the mean RT value of ten test trials.

The overall plan of the experiment is shown in Table 11. The values of the overall means for C_1 and C_2 indicate the difference between hand and foot reaction time.

Apparatus
In testing reaction time the basic essentials for measurement are that the time between the onset of a stimulus, which is under the control of the experimenter, and the onset of the response of the subject to that stimulus, is measured. The stimulus in this experiment is a visual one – the lighting up of an electric light bulb. This may be coloured red or green if you wish to simulate the driving situation more closely. The

Table 11 Plan of hand and foot RT experiment

C_1 – Hand reaction		C_2 – Foot reaction	
S_1 10 test trials		S_9 10 test trials	
S_2	,, ,,	S_{10}	,, ,,
S_3	,, ,,	S_{11}	,, ,,
S_4	,, ,,	S_{12}	,, ,,
S_5	,, ,,	S_{13}	,, ,,
S_6	,, ,,	S_{14}	,, ,,
S_7	,, ,,	S_{15}	,, ,,
S_8	,, ,,	S_{16}	,, ,,
	$\bar{X}$		$\bar{X}$

response required of the subject is to press a push-button or switch, which may be in the form of a pedal, for example. The time between the onset of the stimulus and the reaction of the subject is measured by a timing mechanism. The apparatus required for this is shown in Figure 10. It consists of an electronic timer, connected to mains electricity and wired into a circuit containing two double push-button switches, one of which is operated by the experimenter, the other by the subject. Another circuit, involving a battery supplying low voltage current to a lamp, which is customarily mounted on a screen, is connected mechanically in parallel to the first. The circuit connections are such that the making of the connection at the experimenter's switch causes the onset of the stimulus – the lighting up of the lamp. This is under the control of the experimenter and is effected by depression of the push-button. This simultaneously activates the timer, which continues to operate until the circuit is broken by the subject making his response of depressing his push-button. The time recorded is the interval between the onset of the signal and the subject's reaction to the signal, and this is the reaction time. The way in which the time interval is visually represented on the electronic timer will depend on the model used. There are two basic types in this respect in current use: on a 'clock analogue' model, the time will be shown as values on a series of clock-like dials, while on a digital timer it will appear as a series of digits. Diagrams of both these types appear in Figure 10b.

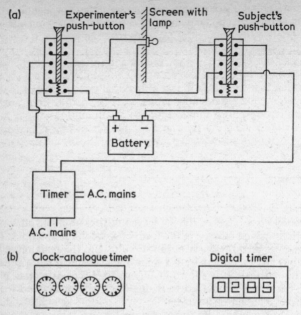

Fig. 10 *Simple reaction time circuit and apparatus*

Procedure

Allocate your subjects to the experimental condition on a random basis, and test each subject individually. Make sure that the spatial arrangement of the apparatus is such that the subject can see the lamp clearly, and has comfortable access to his switch, but *cannot* see the timer, or the experimenter manipulating his switch – this would enable the subject to anticipate the occurrence of a signal and produce a spuriously fast reaction. In your instructions to the subject explain the nature of the task, and motivate him to produce his personal fastest reactions.

A typical trial – a single test of reaction time – will involve the following sequence of events. The subject sits with his hand in a comfortable responding condition, that is, elbow resting on the table, fingers resting lightly on the switch. In this position hand movement time (to the switch) is eliminated, and RT is minimized. If the foot reaction is under test, the subject should find a comfortable responding position for this, heel resting on the floor, toes on the switch. Ask your subject to remove his shoe – this will improve tactile sensitivity and help to preserve the apparatus from damage. Ask your subject to use his preferred hand or foot for the reaction; this will normally, but not necessarily, be the dominant hand or the foot on that side. It is in fact immaterial which hand or foot is used, provided that all the subjects use the defined limb; using the preferred limb should produce the minimum RT.

Before presenting the signal, attract the subject's attention to the imminence of the signal by saying 'Ready' or something to that effect. To obtain maximal preparedness of the subject, and hence the minimal RT, the interval between warning and presentation of the signal should vary between 1 and 4 seconds. It cannot be constant for all trials, since the subject would learn to predict the timing, and react to the time interval instead of to the stimulus. Warning intervals shorter than one second do not allow sufficient time for the subject to build up his preparatory set, while subjects cannot maintain the concentrated attention required for longer than 4 seconds.

Present the stimulus by depressing your switch. This must be done silently otherwise the subject will respond to the auditory stimulus and this will yield spuriously short RTs. After the subject has made his response, record the reading on the timer and re-set the equipment to zero in preparation for the next trial. The inter-trial interval – the interval between the end of one trial and the beginning of the next – should be about 20 seconds, allowing the subject some time for relaxation.

Each subject undergoes ten test trials of this nature.

Do not give your subject any knowledge of results during the experiment; feedback of this sort may have a motivational effect on the subject, improving RT performance, but since the effect is unlikely to be equal for all subjects, it will introduce an unwanted additional source of variance into the data.

The test trials should be preceded by practice trials during which the subject can become accustomed to the equipment and procedure and RTs can stabilize. The results of the practice trials do not, of course, contribute to the subject's RT score, but they can provide an interesting source of data about the way in which practice affects RT.

Anticipatory reactions may occur in the test trials. Although the subject is required to respond at the onset of the stimulus, highly motivated subjects may produce anticipatory reactions by pressing the switch just before the stimulus onset. If the anticipation is considerable, so that the overt response is completed before stimulus onset, the fact that it was an anticipatory reaction will be self-evident. But if the anticipation is only fractional, there will be no clear indication that the reaction was an anticipatory one, apart from a rather short RT. You should therefore treat very short RTs with suspicion, discarding any that are below, say, 160 milliseconds, because they are unlikely to be true RTs.

In order to discover whether a subject is prone to producing anticipatory reactions, include a few 'catch' trials interspersed at random in the series of test trials. A 'catch' trial consists of the *warning* that a stimulus is imminent, but *no* stimulus presentation. If the subject makes a reaction in such a trial, then there are grounds to suspect that some of his other reactions were anticipatory, yielding false RTs, and the data of such a subject should be discarded.

6.3 Treatment of results

From the ten test trials on each subject, you will have obtained ten values of RT. The score required for analysis is the *mean* of these ten values. Calculate this mean RT score for each subject, and enter it into a table of results such as is shown in Table 12.

Calculate the overall mean RT value for each condition. These two values will indicate whether a difference between hand and foot RTs exists, and the direction of the difference. To test whether any apparent difference is due to chance, or to a real difference between hand and foot RTs in general, the data must be subjected to statistical analysis. The analysis appropriate to these data is an unrelated *t*-test, which is appropriate for the following reasons: the experimental design is based on two independent conditions, giving rise to two sets of unrelated scores, and the data are drawn from a continuous distribution of RT values. (A8, Chapter 4.) If you use the data of Table 12 in an unmodified form, one assumption underlying the *t*-test – that of a normal distribution of the dependent variable – will be violated, since the distribution of RTs is slightly skewed, with relatively too few very short ones, and too many long ones. RT data can be normalized by a logarith-

Table 12 Hand and foot RTs in milliseconds

C_1 – *Hand reaction*	C_2 – *Foot reaction*
S_1	S_9
S_2	S_{10}
S_3	S_{11}
S_4	S_{12}
S_5	S_{13}
S_6	S_{14}
S_7	S_{15}
S_8	S_{16}
$\bar{X}$	$\bar{X}$

The score for each subject is the mean RT for ten test trials.

mic transformation of the scores, and this should be done in order to be absolutely correct in applying the t-test. However, the t-test is fairly robust to minor violations of its underlying assumptions, so that in this case you may use it on untransformed RT scores provided that you report the fact, and are aware of its implications. (A8, Chapter 4.)

Since a specific hypothesis was proposed at the beginning of the experiment predicting a directional difference between hand and foot RTs, the unrelated t-test will be one-tailed.

There are other statistical methods by which the data may be analysed, for example, the Mann-Whitney U-test. (A8, Chapter 4.) Since this is a non-parametric test, this will certainly not demand normalization of data through logarithmic transformation, but it is less sensitive than a t-test to the informational content of the data, is less powerful, and therefore has a lower probability of reaching significance.

6.4 Interpretation of results

If the analysis reveals a significant difference in RTs between the two experimental conditions, indicating a significant effect of the independent variable on RT, and the mean value for hand reaction (C_1) is lower than that for foot reaction (C_2), the experiment provides support for the hypothesis that hand RTs are shorter than foot RTs.

It may be that the outcome of the analysis is significant, but the mean RT for hand reactions is *greater* than the mean RT for foot reaction. This will still indicate a significant effect of the independent variable on RT, but the experimental prediction will not be supported.

If the outcome of the analysis does not reach significance, then any apparent differences in RT between the conditions cannot be attributed to the effect of the independent variable, and the experimental hypothesis must be rejected.

6.5 Discussion points

If the results fail to support the hypothesis, consider any aspect of the experimental procedure which could have contributed to this absence of a difference between hand and foot RTs; for example, the subjects performing the foot reaction may have been in an uncomfortable position preventing them from giving their optimal RT performance. Inspect the data of each subject for any peculiarities which could have led to similar overall means for the two conditions; for example, a subject in the hand reaction condition may have produced excessively long RTs, which would have had the effect of raising the mean hand RT value and of reducing the difference between the conditions. The problem of highly atypical scores can be overcome by the use of a large number of subjects, decreasing the weighting of an individual subject's performance in that condition.

If the analysis reveals a significant difference between the conditions, possible causes of this difference other than the main variable of hand or foot reaction should be sought before the hypothesis that there is a difference between hand and foot RT is accepted. One potential cause of this pattern of data lies in differential effects of practice on hand and foot RTs. The general effect of practice is to reduce RT, but it could be that hand RTs require less practice to reach a minimal, stabilized level than foot RTs. If subjects in both conditions receive the same amount of practice in terms of number of trials, hand RTs may be at the optimal level at the beginning of the test trials, while foot RTs may continue to decrease without reaching their 'true' level even by the end of the trials. This would result in invalid measures of foot RTs of too great a length, and would increase the apparent difference between hand and foot RTs.

The same argument may be applied in the opposite direction – that a *failure* to obtain the predicted difference is due to differential practice effects favouring *foot* reactions. On an intuitive basis, this appears to be the less plausible of the two arguments. Whether any support exists for either may be apparent from the inspection of raw data – the RTs of individual subjects on practice and test trials. Allowing for trial to trial fluctuations, a trend of decreasing values throughout the sequence of trials indicates a continuation of practice effects and hence the failure to stabilize performance through practice. Future experiments may be improved in this respect by replacing 'number of practice trials' by 'stability of RT performance' as a criterion of standardization of practice across experimental conditions.

If the experimental hypothesis that hand RTs are shorter than foot RTs can be accepted, an exploration of the effect should be sought in terms of the underlying mechanisms. One possibility is that the difference in RTs may be attributed to the difference in neural conduction time involved in hand and foot reactions, arising from the location of the limbs at different distances from the brain. Assuming the difference in distances involved to be $\frac{1}{2}$ metre, and speed of neural conduction to be 80 metres/second, the difference in neural conduction time for hand and foot reactions is approximately 6 milliseconds. This is so minute a proportion of total reaction time, that although it may be a contributory factor, it is unlikely to play a significant role in the emergence of hand and foot RT differences of the order necessary to reach statistical significance in a laboratory experiment of this design.

Differences between the limbs in the degree of practice as instruments in making finely controlled reactions may be another factor contributing to the difference in RTs, for the hand is used for such responses far more frequently than the foot in everyday life. Furthermore, the musculature and nerve supply of the hand may make it structurally more suitable and more efficient than the foot in the immediate execution of response commands from the brain centres.

Finally, experimental results supporting the hypothesis may have important practical implications. For example, cars of the future may be designed with foot-operated steering, and have braking mechanisms, in which safety considerations make fast reactions of paramount importance, under hand control. Perhaps such a design would be instrumental in decreasing accidents in fog, in which failure to make a braking response with sufficient alacrity is a major factor.

In this context the experimental reaction time data takes on an interesting aspect – whether the reaction times of subjects who are drivers, and therefore accustomed to making fast foot responses during braking, emerge as the fastest in the foot reaction condition. Such an analysis may engender further ideas which can form an expanding basis of enquiry; the effect of car driving on foot reaction time is just one interesting subject.

Experiment 7
Visual search

7.1 Theoretical background

The early parts of this introduction aim to provide a historical perspective to current issues, illustrating in particular the cyclic changes which occur in psychological theory and research.

One of the earliest ideas in experimental psychology, prevalent before the turn of the century, was that the time between a stimulus and the response to it was occupied by a chain of 'mental', or cognitive, processes, such as perception, discrimination, response selection. That is, a reaction time (RT, see Experiment 6) was assumed to be made up of a sequence of component times, each representing the duration of a particular process. This engendered the idea – classically exemplified in the studies of Donders (1868), the Dutch physiologist – that the study of reaction time could be used to reveal information about the underlying processes. Donders used three basic reaction situations, which have become known as Donders' a, b and c reactions, and these are shown in Figure 11. Reaction a was a simple RT situation, involving only one possible stimulus and one response to that stimulus (e.g. a red light as stimulus requiring a key to be pressed with the right hand), and was thought to be composed of perception and response execution. Reaction b was a choice RT, involving two possible stimuli, each requiring a different response from the other (e.g. red or blue light, requiring a response with the left or right hand, respectively). This reaction was thought to be composed of simple RT, plus *discrimination* of which stimulus had occurred, plus *response selection* of the appropriate response. In reaction *c* there were two possible stimuli (e.g. red and blue light) but a response was required to only one of them (e.g. pressing a key with the left hand to the red light). This was thought to involve simple RT plus discrimination, but *no* response selection, since there was only one possible response. By measuring reaction times in these three reaction situations, and by algebraic manipulation of the data, as shown in Figure 11, Donders sought to establish the exact duration of each of the processes involved.

Reaction	S–R relations	Cognitive processes involved
Donders' a	S_1–R_1	Perception and response (simple RT).
Donders' b	S_1–R_1	RT + discrimination
	S_2–R_2	+ response selection.
Donders' c 'Go–no go' reaction	S_1–R_1	RT + discrimination.
	S_2	

E.g. discrimination time $= c - a$
response selection $= b - a - c$

Wundt's d	$\begin{matrix} S_1 \\ \\ S_2 \end{matrix}\Big\rangle R$	RT + discrimination.

Fig. 11 *Types of reaction situations*

Wundt, a German psychologist, was quick to point to a fault in Donders' reasoning: that reaction *c* did involve response selection, that of whether to make or to refrain from making a response. In an attempt to rectify this, Wundt introduced a *d* reaction, also shown in Figure 11, in which the same response was to be given to whichever of two stimuli occurred, the subject being instructed to respond *after* he had discriminated which stimulus had occurred. An obvious criticism of the *d* reaction is that the subject may choose not to, or may be unable to, wait until after discriminating before beginning to make his response. That is, there would be some overlap between discrimination time and response selection time.

After enjoying considerable popularity, problems with this method of research became apparent. The underlying logic was in some cases dubious; large variations, including some *negative* times, were found for particular processes; introspective reports did not support the theory of *sequences* of processing. The root of the problem was the total reliance on the assumption of a non-overlapping sequence of processing: that only when one stage of processing is completed does the next one commence. While this assumption *may* be valid, the possibility of it being invalid renders any attempt to calculate the precise duration of any process meaningless. Thus, the research fell into disrepute and faded into obscurity for over half a century.

Recent years have seen a revival of the use of temporal characteristics of performance as a means of insight into the processes of information analysis underlying that performance. The revival is probably due to the adoption of a less rigid approach; whereas early work concentrated on isolating and timing single stages of processing, contemporary research seeks to describe and interpret variations in response time as a function of changes in the task required of the subject. That is, while the early work was based on an assumption of 'pure insertion' (that a change in the task caused the addition or subtraction of a processing stage, without altering others), contemporary work is based on an assumption of 'selective influence' (that a change in the task will alter the *duration* of some stage, which will be evident by a change in reaction time, without altering others).

One area of research exemplifying the use of temporal characteristics of performance in investigations of processes underlying that performance is that of visual pattern recognition. The work of Neisser (1964, 1967) provides an excellent example of this approach.

Neisser devised a simple task in which the speed of searching for a particular visual pattern in a sequence of patterns is measured. The task involves the subject searching through a list of items, typically letters of the alphabet, for a pre-defined target item, e.g. the letter A. A typical arrangement of the search list is a column of about fifty rows, with about four letters per row, as shown in Figure 12.

The target letter in this list is A:

EHYP
SWIQ
UFCJ
WBYH
OGTX
GWXV
TWLN
XJBU
UDXI
HSFP
XSCQ
SDJU
ZVBP
PODC
PEVZ
SLRK
JCEN
ZLRD
XBOD
PHMU
ZHFA
PNJW
CQXT
GHNR
IXYD
QSVB
GUCH
OWBN
BVQN
FOKS

Fig. 12 *Example of a visual search list (after Neisser)*

The subject's task is to scan down the list row by row, as quickly as possible, starting at the top left-hand corner, until he finds the target letter, when he makes a response; this usually consists of pressing a key, which is connected to a timer, and the total search time, from the beginning to the location of the target, is thus measured and recorded. This is the time taken to process all the items in the list up to and including the target item, plus actual movement time to make the response. The search speed (time to process a single item) can be found approximately by dividing the total search time by the number of items processed.

The position of the target in the list is varied from trial to trial, so that search times involving a varying number of items can be obtained. Figure 13 shows typical results presented by Neisser from such an experiment.

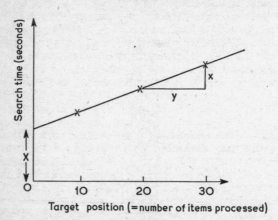

Fig. 13 *Example of typical results in a visual search task*

The function is linear, indicating that the search rate is constant – it does not decrease or increase as the search continues. The intercept (X) provides a measure of the motor response time – this exists even with zero items to be processed, and will depend on the individual's reaction time, the nature of the apparatus, etc., but will not be related to the visual processing rate. The slope of the function, x/y, provides a measure of search time per item, i.e. the search rate. Neisser found that typical search rates were of the order of 40 milliseconds per item, but varied with the nature of the search task.

One of the factors affecting search rate is the context in which the target is embedded. For example, if the target letter A is embedded in a list of visually similar letters (e.g. X, Y, V) search rates are slower than if it is embedded in a list of letters dissimilar to itself (e.g. B, C, S).

These variations in rate for searches involving different visual patterns suggest that the processes underlying the searches differ according to the information to be processed, which may throw tentative light on the way in which analysis and recognition of visual patterns occurs. Pursuing this line of thought, Neisser has proposed that his data suggest, or at least are in accord with, a particular model of visual pattern recognition, based on the detection of individual elements of a form. This model is embedded in a major theory of pattern recognition – the feature-analysis theory.

The feature-analysis theory holds that patterns are recognized on the basic of combinations of particular characteristics or features which they possess. It presupposes (not without evidence) that there exists a system of mechanisms, or feature-analysers, which are sensitive to and detect specific elements or features of visual form. These features are undefined by the theory, but at a simple conceptual level they may be straight vertical and horizontal lines, curves, etc. More complex patterns consist of a particular combination of certain basic features – for example, the letter A is made up of three straight lines at different orientation. When a feature or combination of features occurs, it evokes a response in the feature-analysers sensitive to it, and the pattern is 'recognized', i.e. the individual is aware of having seen the pattern before.

Feature-analysis theory contrasts with another theory of pattern recognition – that of template-matching. Template-matching claims that whenever a visual pattern is encountered, a model, blueprint, or *template*, of it is set up within the perceptual system. When the pattern is encountered subsequently a comparison is made with existing templates, and if a match occurs the pattern is 'recognized'. One of the criticisms of template-matching is that it appears to require a vast store of templates to account for numerous slight variations in a pattern which are recognized as basically the same pattern. For example, a sample of handwritten letter A's will vary greatly in visual form, but most people experience no difficulty in recognizing them all as A's.

The critical difference between the two theories is that pattern recognition is hypothesized to occur on a holistic basis according to template-matching, and by a synthesis of elements according to feature-analysis. Feature-analysis proposes a more flexible mode of pattern perception, in that it does not demand identity of patterns on different occasions in order that recognition should occur – it is sufficient that general *characteristics* be present. Furthermore, it can accommodate a hierarchical system of pattern analysis, with simple feature-analysers operating at the lowest level, e.g. detectors of straight lines, and more complex, higher order analysers being sensitive to particular combinations of activation of basic analysers (e.g. detectors of the pattern H).

The thesis that Neisser's work supports feature-analysis as a model of pattern recognition rests on several aspects of his findings, but the one relevant to this experiment is the fact that search rates for targets embedded in visually similar contexts are slower than those for targets embedded in dissimilar contexts. Such context effects would not be predicted on the basis of template-matching; since each item in the list would be analysed fully and tested against a template of the target before it could be rejected as a non-target item (or accepted as the target), the degree of similarity between the item and the target should be of no consequence. These context effects, however, can be readily accommodated within the feature-analysis model, assuming some form of hierarchical processing. For instance, when target and contextual items are similar, target and non-target items will have some features in common which will activate the same feature-analysers, e.g. a target letter L and a context of T's will all activate feature-analysers for | and — elements. Therefore, the analysis of each non-target item has to be continued to a level beyond that of simple features, a level involving analysers sensitive to relationships between features. Thus a relatively long time will be devoted to each item before it can be discarded and the search continued. When target and contextual items are dissimilar, they will have few features in common, and non-target items can be discarded very early in their analysis, on the basis that they fail to activate analysers for basic features of the target item. A shorter time is required per item in this case, and search rates will be faster than those for targets embedded in similar contexts.

This is perhaps an appropriate point at which to take a retrospective and summarizing glance at the preceding paragraphs. An old idea and experimental approach to the analysis of information processing – that of using temporal characteristics of performance as a means of insight into the underlying processes – has undergone a renaissance, and is proving a highly stimulating and productive tool of research in its modified contemporary form.

The present experiment continues in this tradition by examining the temporal characteristics of visual search. It aims to extend the investigation of contextual effects on search rate to three degrees of target-context similarity, in the hope that this may further our knowledge about the way in which visual information is processed. In the light of past research, it is possible to predict that the greater the degree of target-context similarity, the slower the search rate.

7.2 Method

Design
The experiment is based on Neisser's search task, where the time to find a pre-defined target letter by scanning down a search list is measured.

The *independent variable* will be the context in which the target is embedded, i.e. the nature of the non-target items, and three levels of this variable are used. That is, there are three different search lists, varying in the degree of similarity between target and contextual items, giving rise to three experimental conditions.

In condition 1 (C_1), the degree of target-context similarity is low (e.g. target A, context C, O, S, U). In condition 3 (C_3), the degree of target-context similarity is high (e.g. target A, context X, Y, V, K). In condition 2 (C_2), the degree of target-context similarity is intermediate (e.g. target A, context C, O, K, V).

Each subject will serve under only *one* of the experimental conditions; this means that the three conditions are *independent*, or *unrelated*. By using an independent groups design certain problems of order of testing subjects and data analysis will be avoided.

The *dependent variable* is the measure of subject's performance – the search rate in each of the three conditions. The predicted effect of the variation in context on search rate is that search rates will become slower (more time per item), as the degree of target-context similarity increases, C_3 producing the slowest rates of search. The experimental hypothesis is therefore that the order of the experimental conditions in terms of search *time* will be $C_1 < C_2 < C_3$.

Measurement of search rate
The search rate can be found for each subject by the method described in the introductory section – that is, search times for

at least three target positions are found and the data represented graphically (Figure 13). The slope of the resulting function gives a measure of time per item, i.e. search rate. Although you are free to adopt this method, it is likely to prove rather laborious. An alternative method and the one recommended for, and adopted in, the description of this experiment is simply to find the search time for a particular target position, and divide it by the number of items processed (number of items up to and including the target). This is rather a crude and distorted measure of search rate, since the total search time will include, in addition to visual processing time, the *reaction time* needed to indicate the finding of the target (intercept X in Figure 13). This reaction time will be roughly constant for all searches, and will increase the estimate of search rate more for fast searches than slow ones, by representing a greater proportion of the total time. Since this controlled, systematic bias of the data will be *against* the predicted effect of contextual similarity, it cannot be instrumental in producing spurious support for the experimental hypothesis, any support will occur *in spite of* the measurement technique. So although this method of estimating search rate, proposed in the interests of simplicity, represents a deliberate confounding of the dependent variable, this can be justified on theoretical grounds of experimental design, and the method may be adopted for use in this experiment. That is, each subject will be tested at one target position, and his search task estimated by dividing total search time by the number of items processed (i.e. target position).

Trials
Since the nature of the task invalidates repeated measures on the same subject using the same target position (the subject will learn where the target is located and can avoid the search), you will only be able to conduct *one* trial per subject. This may seem rather wasteful in terms of subjects, and detract from the reliability of the data, but it seems to be the optimal solution within the bounds of the nature of the experiment. It does mean that you will need a large number of subjects to achieve reliability and stability of data.

Target position
Although each subject is to contribute one score, obtained from a single search, to the final data, the length of that search

(i.e. target position in list) should not be constant for all subjects. If it were, then the findings would be subject to the criticism that they are specific to that particular length of search task and do not provide a reliable basis for generalization. One solution is complete randomization of target positions across all subjects, but this would create considerable hardship in the construction of search lists. Therefore, only three target positions have been chosen: T_1, T_2 and T_3, and these are evenly distributed within and across conditions. That is, within a condition, T_1 will be used for the same number of subjects as T_2 and T_3, and this will be repeated exactly for all conditions. The minimum number of subjects needed in each target position is probably four, giving a total of twelve subjects per condition, thirty-six subjects in all, though the more subjects you use in this experiment, the better.

The overall design of the experiment, showing distribution of subjects and target positions in the three experimental conditions, is shown in Table 13.

Table 13 General plan of the experimental design

| Target position | Experimental conditions (degree of target-context similarity). | | |
	C_1	C_2	C_3
T_1	S_1	S_{13}	S_{25}
	S_2	S_{14}	S_{26}
	S_3	S_{15}	S_{27}
	S_4	S_{16}	S_{28}
T_2	S_5	S_{17}	S_{29}
	S_6	S_{18}	S_{30}
	S_7	S_{19}	S_{31}
	S_8	S_{20}	S_{32}
T_3	S_9	S_{21}	S_{33}
	S_{10}	S_{22}	S_{34}
	S_{11}	S_{23}	S_{35}
	S_{12}	S_{24}	S_{36}

Each subject (S) contributes one score – his search rate achieved on one trial at his target position.

The fact that three target positions are used per condition means that the search data can be depicted graphically, making them comparable to other research (Figure 13). The search *time* at each of the target positions, averaged over the subjects tested at that target position, can be plotted against the number of items processed, for each of the three experimental conditions. This is shown in Figure 14, the three functions being drawn on the basis of the experimental prediction – that search rate will be slower with increasing target-context similarity. Before looking at Figure 14, see if *you* can predict how the graphs for each condition should appear. Bear in mind that search *times* are bound to increase with search length (from T_1 to T_3), and that search times include the final reaction time involved in making the indicating response.

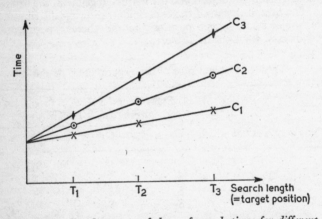

Fig. 14 *Predicted pattern of data of search times for different search lengths, in the three experimental conditions*
Each point on the graph would be the mean of four subjects' scores

Structure of search lists
This section describes some very specific search lists, which are shown in Appendix III.

(i) The basic structure of the search lists is a column consisting of eighty rows of letters, with four letters per row.

(ii) Three lists are needed for each experimental condition, one for each of the three target positions. The actual target positions selected are the 100th, 200th and 300th item as T_1,

T_2 and T_3 respectively; that is, the target appears on or just after the 25th, 50th and 75th row of the list. The position is not always *exactly* the 100th, 200th or 300th item since this would cause the target always to appear at the end of a row, which could lead to spuriously early identification.

Computation of the search rates may still be based on target positions of 100, 200 and 300, since the slight deviation from the exact theoretical positions will be of little consequence because of the large numerical values involved. The choice of target positions has not been entirely arbitrary; it is based on the minimum search time that can be accurately recorded, and the maximal duration of searches feasible in the time usually available for a laboratory experiment.

(iii) The target item in all conditions is the letter A. Non-target items have been chosen on an intuitive basis as fulfilling the required similarity relations to the target. In C_1 the non-target items are C, O, S, and U. In C_3 they are K, V, X and Y. In C_2 half are drawn from C_1, half from C_3, and they are C, O, K and V. The sequence of contextual items has been randomized row by row, so that all four items appear in each non-target-containing row. The position of the target item within a row, approximating to the theoretically required target position, has also been selected on a random basis.

(iv) The search lists for each condition are shown in Appendix III. The target item has been inserted into all three target positions, T_1, T_2 and T_3, in each list. You will have to prepare your own lists for use in experimentation, inserting a target only into the relevant target position in each list, and replacing the two redundant targets with the contextual letters appropriate to that line. Make sure that the items are clearly and evenly printed in capitals; use a typewriter if possible. It is essential that the list be in the form of *one long continuous column*; you will have to use long strips of paper, possibly glueing several together, to obtain the desired length. If the list were broken up into several columns, as are the ones in Appendix III, the time required for eye movements across the columns would introduce an uncontrolled confounding variable into the measure of search time.

(v) The lists described here have been constructed to help with some of the preparation for the experiment, but you can construct your own lists, deviating from these in terms of target position, total length of list, number of letters per row, and identity of letters used as contextual and target items, provided that they conform to the general theoretical demands of the experimental design.

Materials for use in the experiment

(i) Nine search lists, as described in the preceding section.

(ii) Several search lists different from above, for use in practice trials. Since each subject receives only one test trial, practice trials are essential to accustom him to the task. Practice lists can be shorter than test lists, and composed of a target and contextual items of your own choice. The search list shown in Figure 12 should provide a good basis for practice lists.

(iii) Blank sheets of paper to cover search lists before the start of a trial.

(iv) A stop watch.

Procedure

This experiment is one that, because of the large number of subjects required, may tempt you to take it out of the laboratory setting, and this is entirely feasible since the equipment involved is simple and easily transportable. If you do decide to conduct it outside the laboratory, make sure that conditions that might affect the subject's performance – such as lighting, seating, social atmosphere, etc. – are as comparable as possible for all subjects, thereby minimizing extraneous sources of variability in the data.

Allocate your subjects to the experimental conditions and target positions on a random basis. The fact that subjects are numbered consecutively in Table 13, showing the overall design of the experiment, does not mean that you *test* the subjects in that order. Decide by some means of randomization which subject number is to be allocated to each fresh subject.

One important point which has not yet been mentioned is that the subject's performance *must be free from error* – he must not detect a false target, nor miss an actual target. Such errors, indicating inaccurate information processing, would obviously render the measure of search time invalid, and that subject's data would have to be discarded. In order to avoid an undue waste of subjects, you must ensure that in your instructions to the subject you convey the need for accurate performance at the maximum speed possible with sufficient gravity to achieve co-operation and compliance in your subjects.

Having explained the task to the subject, including instructions to start the search at the top left-hand corner of the list and scan down it, give the subject a few practice trials to accustom him to the task, followed by the test trial.

Each trial should proceed along the following lines: the subject sits with the search list, covered by a blank sheet of paper, in front of him. His eyes should be focused on a point in the top centre of the cover, where the top of the search list will appear, and his hand held in readiness to indicate the target. The experimenter swiftly removes the cover, simultaneously starting the stop watch. The subject scans down the list until he locates the target, which he indicates by saying 'Here' or something to that effect, and pointing to it. The verbal indication will be the faster, and as soon as he hears this the experimenter stops the stop watch, on which the total search time will be shown. Record the search time to the nearest fraction of a second shown on your stop watch.

This is, admittedly, rather a crude method of timing the search, since the subject's search time will be 'contaminated' by the experimenter's reaction time in starting and stopping the stop watch. This additional source of variance can be minimized by the experimenter being very well practiced in his task, and responding consistently with his minimum reaction time. This will then form a *constant* addition to the time recorded and will not bias a particular experimental group.

7.3 Treatment of results

(i) You will have a measure of search *time* for each subject; enter this into a table such as shown in Table 14. You will probably find large variations in the scores, but there should be a general trend of increasing scores *down* the columns, i.e. from T_1 to T_3.

Find the *mean value* of search times at each target position – e.g. for C_1, T_1, mean value of scores from S_1, S_2, S_3 and S_4 is denoted by $\bar{x}_1$. You will need these values to represent the data graphically. Find the overall mean $(\bar{X})$ for each condition.

(ii) The primary aim of the experiment is to examine the effect of degree of target-context similarity on search *rate*, and this is the measure of performance needed for statistical analysis of the data. Find the search rate for each subject by dividing the search time by the number of items processed

Table 14 Table of search times, in seconds

	Experimental conditions		
	C_1	C_2	C_3
Target position T_1	S_1	S_{13}	S_{25}
	S_2	S_{14}	S_{26}
	S_3	S_{15}	S_{27}
	S_4	S_{16}	S_{28}
	$\bar{x}_1$	$\bar{x}_4$	$\bar{x}_7$
T_2	S_5	S_{17}	S_{29}
	S_6	S_{18}	S_{30}
	S_7	S_{19}	S_{31}
	S_8	S_{20}	S_{32}
	$\bar{x}_2$	$\bar{x}_5$	$\bar{x}_8$
T_3	S_9	S_{21}	S_{33}
	S_{10}	S_{22}	S_{34}
	S_{11}	S_{23}	S_{35}
	S_{12}	S_{24}	S_{36}
	$\bar{x}_3$	$\bar{x}_6$	$\bar{x}_9$
	$\bar{X}_1$	$\bar{X}_2$	$\bar{X}_3$

(100 in T_1, 200 in T_2 and 300 in T_3). Enter the search rates into a table such as is shown in Table 15. To eliminate decimal values you can multiply all scores by some common factor, e.g. 100. Note that the target position information has now been disregarded. Find the mean value of search rate in each experimental condition. This will provide some indication of whether the data fit the experimental prediction – that search rate becomes slower with an increase in the degree of target-context similarity. If they do, then the value for the search rate will increase from C_1 to C_3.

(iii) Analysis. In order to determine whether the data of Table 14 do support the experimental hypothesis, they must be subjected to statistical analysis. The appropriate analysis for these data is a Jonckheere Trend test (A8, Ch. 6) which is applicable to three or more independent groups of scores, and specifically tests whether there is a trend in one direction across the groups.

(If you are proficient in more sophisticated techniques of analysis, you could subject the data to an analysis of variance,

Table 15 Search rate data

C_1	C_2	C_3
S_1	S_{13}	S_{25}
S_2	S_{14}	S_{26}
S_3	S_{15}	S_{27}
S_4	S_{16}	S_{28}
S_5	S_{17}	S_{29}
S_6	S_{18}	S_{30}
S_7	S_{19}	S_{31}
S_8	S_{20}	S_{32}
S_9	S_{21}	S_{33}
S_{10}	S_{22}	S_{34}
S_{11}	S_{23}	S_{35}
S_{12}	S_{24}	S_{36}
$\bar{X}_1$	$\bar{X}_2$	$\bar{X}_3$

which would indicate whether there are any significant *differences* between the experimental conditions, and the directional trend could be tested using a linear comparison.)

7.4 Interpretation of results

If the outcome of your analysis is significant, then your data indicate that the context in which a target is embedded does affect the search rate, the specific effect being to slow search rate down as target-context similarity increases.

There is still one aspect of the data which has not been considered, and that is the variable of target position. The data relevant to this are the search times in Table 14. Using the mean search time for each target position (i.e. x_1, x_2, etc.) plot the relationship between time and the number of items processed at each target position (i.e. 100, 200 or 300), for each experimental condition. The resulting graph will have three lines on it, one representing each experimental condition. The position and shape of these lines is a valuable source of information about the processes underlying the search. A straight line indicates that the search speed is constant through-out the duration of the search. If a line is curved, the direction of the curve will indicate the change in the rate of search. In Figure 15, line *a* denotes a constant search rate, line *b* denotes a search speeding up as it continues, and line c denotes a search slowing down as it continues. None of the functions should pass through the origin of the graph, since there is always a minimum response time, even with zero items to be processed.

If your statistical analysis of search rates indicates a significant effect of target-context similarity, and in view of earlier

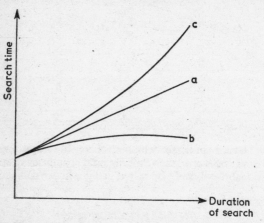

Fig. 15 *Hypothetical functions relating search rate to duration of search*

research findings that search speeds are usually constant, you may find that your graph of search time versus search length is somewhat similar to the one shown in Figure 16. The lines representing the three experimental conditions should have approximately the same intercept on the 'time' axis, indicating that there are no gross differences in subject and experimenter response time between the conditions.

The search rate is given by the slope of the function relating time to number of items processed, i.e. t/n. C_1, with the fastest search rate, should have the lowest slope (relatively little time per item). The slope of C_2 should be steeper, and the slope of C_3 steepest of all. The estimates of search rate obtained from the graph (i.e. t_1/n_1, t_2/n_2, t_3/n_3) should correspond approximately to the mean search rate for each condition obtained in Table 15. Any deviations from the pattern of data shown in Figure 16 should provide you with an interesting source of

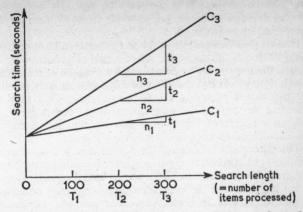

Fig. 16 *Predicted relationship between search times and search length*
Each point is the mean of four subjects' search time.
The search rate is given by t_1/n_1 in C_1 t_2/n_2 in C_2 t_3/n_3 in C_3

speculation and interpretation of the underlying cause and significance.

(If you are proficient with more sophisticated techniques of analysis, the variable of target position, of which no account is taken in the Jonckheere Trend test, can be analysed by using a two-way analysis of variance. The relevant data are the search *times* in Table 14, and the two variables are the degree of target-context similarity (three levels: C_1, C_2 and C_3) and target position (with three levels: T_1, T_2 and T_3), giving rise to a 3×3 cell matrix with four subjects in each cell.)

7.5 Discussion points

Before accepting and interpreting the outcome of the experiment, whether it supports or fails to support the hypothesis, consider possible criticisms of the design and procedure and possible factors other than that of the independent variable, which could have given rise to the pattern of data obtained. For example, only one target letter was used throughout the experiment, and only a small selection of contextual items. This lays the experiment open to the criticism that the results are specific to the particular characteristics of the items used, and may not be applicable in general. To test this hypothesis another experiment is needed, in which identity of target and contextual items is varied.

Failure to achieve support for the experimental hypothesis could be due to the deliberate introduction of a controlled bias against the hypothesis by employing a technique of measuring search time which had the effect of disproportionately increasing the values recorded for faster searches. This may be remedied by varying the target position for each subject, so that an estimate of search rate can be obtained from the graphical representation of each subject's data.

The theoretical context of the experiment is that of using temporal characteristics of performance in seeking insight into the processes involved in visual search and the perception of visual patterns, and the experimental findings may be related to and interpreted in these terms. For example, a plausible interpretation of the search rate being adversely affected by increasing target-context similarity is that the process of analysing visual information up to the point at which a decision to reject non-target items can be taken takes longer when there are more elements or features in common between target and contextual items. It is this sort of reasoning that has led to the interpretation of contextual effects on search rate as evidence for a feature-analysis, as opposed to a holistic, template-matching, model of pattern recognition. For, according to a template-matching model, each non-target is fully analysed before rejection, and the time required to complete the analysis would be the same, regardless of the degree of the item's similarity to the target. However, the contextual similarity effect *can* be accommodated by template-matching if the search process is assumed to involve, in addition to complete visual pattern analysis, a matching and decision stage. During this stage each pattern would be tested against a template of the target, and be accepted as the target or rejected as a non-target item, depending on whether a match occurred or not. It could be that the increase in search time due to greater target-context similarity arises not from a deeper analysis of non-target items, as is proposed by proponents of feature-analysis theory, but from an increase in difficulty associated with the matching, testing and decision-making process. The relative validity of this and previously described views of the search process are open to experimental test, using methods similar to the one employed in this experiment.

It seems that this whole area of research into information processing utilizing temporal characteristics of performance has many unexplored possibilities and is a fertile field for future endeavour.

Experiment 8
Colour, brain waves and the experience of time

8.1 Theoretical background

The study of time has been of interest to many disciplines of learning – physics, philosophy, geology, mathematics – for centuries, and the perception of time was one of the first subjects to be investigated in the dawn of experimental psychology. These early studies led by Titchener in the U.S.A. and Wundt in Germany at the turn of the last century were based on subjective introspection as a method of research and fell into disrepute with the rise of Behaviorism which emphasized the objective study of overt behaviour.

Subsequent research was more empirical in approach, but rather fragmentary, due to the lack of any unifying theory of time perception; it was of a prosaic nature (Woodrow 1951) and failed for over fifty years to stimulate any widespread interest in the area.

Underlying much research was an implicit assumption that time exists as an independent dimension in the universe, analogous to light or sound, and therefore that the perception of time is a sensory process analogous to other sensory processes such as visual or auditory perception. A frequent but even more misguided assumption was that this 'real' time was measured by the clock time of Western convention, and this led to a concentration of research on factors affecting accuracy of time perception with respect to clock time. Clock time, with its units of seconds, minutes and hours, is no more a representation of 'real' time than units of 'how long an egg takes to boil'; it is merely a convenient way of organizing a life overcrowded with events.

This conceptualization of time led to the postulation of, and the search for, a mechanism of time perception – a sensory organ of time, an internal biological clock, which would lie at the basis of the experience of time. This mechanism was often envisaged either as a counter-device, noting the number of events of some sort, or a pulse-dispensing mechanism delivering signals at regular intervals which would serve as the foundation for time experience.

Typical of the research arising from this theoretical context and seeking to implicate a physiological process in time per-ception is the work of Hoagland (1933). He believed that time perception was related to, and possibly mediated by, body temperature; the higher the body temperature, the faster the rate at which time appeared to pass in relation to clock time. For instance, a subject with a raised body temperature (caused by influenza), attempting to count up to 60 at the rate of one a second, would count more quickly, reaching 60 before a minute of clock time had passed, than when his body temperature was normal.

A variety of physiological processes have been postulated to lie at the basis of time experience – heart rate, thyroid activity, metabolic rate, brain cell activity (recorded as waves on the electro-encephalograph – EEG), provide but a small sample. Although there is no doubt that biological rhythms do exist and are probably under the control of neural structures in the higher centres of the brain, since their rhythmic variations are not correlated, it is difficult to accept them all as *the* mediator of time perception.

A breakaway from these lines of thought was made by Ornstein (1969) whose ideas are rooted in the premise that time has no independent existence in the universe. His thesis is that the experience of time is a mental construction – a cognitive concept – created from the events which occur during the life of an individual. The idea is not novel – it had been suggested by Guyau (1890), for example, but had lain dormant for decades. Specifically, Ornstein's proposal was his 'storage size' hypothesis – that experience of duration is directly proportional to the amount of cortical space occupied by the analysis and storage of incoming events, both number of events and perceived complexity of events being factors affecting storage space.

The storage size metaphor received support from a series of experimental findings. For example, subjects were asked to listen to three tape recordings of short tones (events) occurring

110

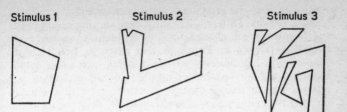

Stimulus 1   Stimulus 2   Stimulus 3

Fig. 17 *Some of the stimuli used by Ornstein*

at irregular intervals; although all tapes were of equal clock time length, the greater the number of events on a tape, the longer the duration of the tape appeared to the subjects. Experience of duration was shown to be similarly affected by visual complexity of stimuli: a series of two-dimensional geometric forms of varying degrees of complexity (see Figure 17) was presented. Although exposure of each stimulus was equated for *clock* duration with all other stimuli, the *subjective* experience of duration increased in relation to increasing complexity of the stimuli.

This, and other evidence, suggests that the experience of time is altered by the number and nature of events. Although the underlying mechanisms are not clear, the thesis that the experience of time is *constructed* by the individual from incoming events is highly plausible and offers a wide and fascinating field of enquiry.

Studies in this field have been based on events of which the subjects were consciously unaware. But the mechanism of construction of time experience does not operate at a level which is open to conscious introspection. There exists, therefore, a hitherto unexplored avenue of research with rather esoteric overtones – that events which do not reach a level of conscious awareness may serve as a basis of time construction and lie at the origin of the conscious experience of duration. A particularly good example of such events, whose existence is well documented at the neurophysiological level but which are not represented at the level of conscious awareness, are the patterns of activity of brain cells. These patterns give rise to varying electrical potentials on the scalp, which can be detected by electrodes and recorded by a machine known as the electro-encephalograph. The term 'EEG rhythm' is frequently applied both to the recordings and to the underlying patterns of brain activity. Different EEG rhythms, varying in amplitude and frequency, are characteristic of different levels of bodily arousal, as shown in Figure 18. For example, beta rhythm, consisting of highly desynchronized waves with a low amplitude and a high frequency (number of cyclic changes per second, measured in Hz units), is associated with a state of excitement. The waves characteristic of deep sleep, delta rhythm, are of large amplitude and low frequency.

Experimentation involving monitoring and analysis of EEG rhythm presents a problem; it requires a degree of sophistication of experimenter and equipment which puts it beyond the scope of a simple psychological experiment. However, if a simple method known to alter EEG rhythm could be found, then the investigation of EEG rhythms as subconscious events lying at the basis of time experience could be realized.

Fortunately, such a method has come to light; there is some evidence that EEG rhythms are affected by the colour of the visual stimulation falling on the individual. Gerard (1958) has shown that red light produces desynchronization of EEG patterns (higher frequency of waves) in comparison with white light, while blue or blue-green light falling on the retina has the opposite effect. The effect on EEG rhythm is inversely proportional to the wavelength of the light, since blue light has the shorter wavelength, 400 nm (nanometers) and red light the longer (700 nm). This is shown diagrammatically in Figure 19.

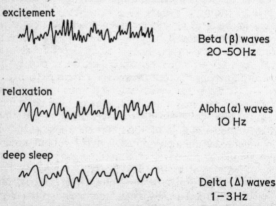

excitement — Beta (β) waves 20-50 Hz

relaxation — Alpha (α) waves 10 Hz

deep sleep — Delta (Δ) waves 1-3 Hz

Fig. 18 *Schematic representation of EEG rhythms*

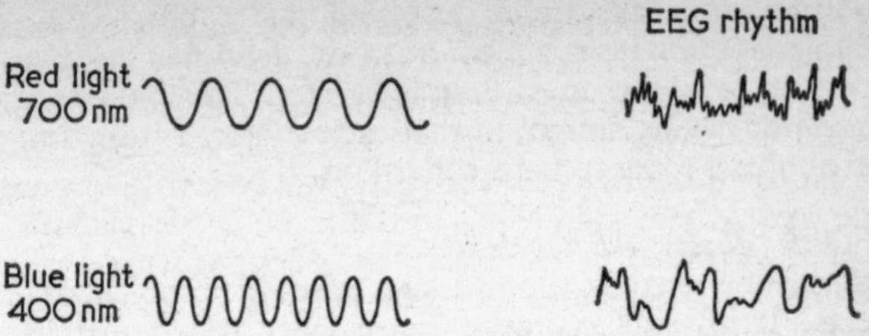

Fig. 19 *Schematic representation of wavelengths of blue and red light, and the effect on EEG rhythm*

This information – that EEG rhythms are altered by the colour of visual stimulation – opens the way to the study of the relationship between subconscious events and the conscious experience of time, with EEG rhythms constituting a specific class of events below the level of conscious awareness.

On the assumption that the role of subconscious events in the construction of time experience is similar to that of conscious events, it may be predicted that the experience of duration under red light will be lengthened in comparison with that under blue. In comparison with blue light, red light will increase the frequency of EEG waves, thereby increasing the number of changes of events occurring within a unit of clock time, and providing the basis for the construction of more 'time'. Therefore, the following experimental hypothesis, couched in concrete terms related to the proposed experimental manipulations, may be put forward: that the duration of time experience will be lengthened under red light in comparison with blue light.

8.2 Method

(i) *Design*
This is probably the most complicated experiment in terms of design and procedural technique, and in order to maximize clarity this section has been divided into a larger number of subsections than usual.

The experimental design involves two conditions, arising from the two values of the *independent variable* – wavelength of light. In condition 1 (C_1), the 'Red' condition, time experience is tested under red light, and in condition 2 (C_2), the 'Blue' condition, time experience is tested under blue light. The technique of obtaining a measure of the *dependent variable*, the experience of duration, is described later. The two conditions are *related* in this design, in that each subject is tested in and contributes a score to both conditions.

(ii) *Order effects, ABBA design*

The use of a related-groups design raises the problem of order effects. If all subjects were consistently tested just in one condition, and then in the other, a systematic bias would be introduced into the experiment, with the results of the condition to be tested second being contaminated by residual effects (e.g. due to tiredness) of the subject first being tested in the other condition (see section 2.2). This would preclude any conclusions being drawn from the experiment, since the independent variable would not be the only consistent source of variance, or difference, between the conditions. A number of solutions to problems of order are available. The *starting* condition for each subject may be randomized, eliminating a systematic bias within the experiment as a whole, although each individual subject's performance will be influenced by order effects. Another solution is to randomize the order of the conditions *trial by trial* for each subject. This eliminates systematic bias from both individual subject's data and the experiment as a whole. However, in the context of this experiment, practical considerations militate against this method of total randomization, for frequent changes of colour of the environment could be difficult to arrange.

The solution to both theoretical and practical problems of order effects adopted in this experiment is a compromise between total randomization and no randomization, and this particular compromise, involving counterbalancing of the order of conditions, is known as an ABBA design. For each subject the total number of trials in the two conditions, A and B, is halved, giving rise to four blocks of trials: A_1, A_2, and B_1, B_2. The experiment is conducted with the blocks of trials in the following order: A_1, B_1, B_2, A_2. In this way an equal section of each condition precedes and follows an equal section of the other condition, and order effects are counterbalanced.

The experimental condition to be designated as A or B is decided on a random basis for each subject – e.g. for one subject A is Red and B is Blue; for another, A may be Blue and B

114

may be Red. The number of trials appropriate to striking a balance between being sufficient for reliable results and not overtiring the subject is twenty, ten trials in each condition. These are divided into the ABBA pattern of blocks, five trials per block. The data from the two blocks of five in each condition are pooled for purposes of subsequent analysis.

(iii) *Measuring the experience of duration*

There are numerous techniques for measuring the experience of time, but many are intrinsically linked with the subject's ability to name or relate to intervals of clock time. The theoretical context of this experiment denies clock time as the basis of time experience, and therefore demands that these techniques be discarded. The technique chosen for this experiment is one adapted from Ornstein (1969), and avoids problems of relating the experience of duration to clock intervals.

The subject is presented with a certain interval of time, which he experiences under *white* light, and this serves as a *standard* with which other intervals may be compared. The duration of the standard is represented visually by a straight horizontal line drawn for the subject on a piece of plain paper. Although this could be drawn by the subject himself, subjects find it easier if a reference relating experience of duration to length of line is provided for them. A *comparison* interval, equal in clock duration to the standard, is then presented under *coloured* light, and the subject indicates the subjective duration of this interval in relation to the standard, by drawing a second horizontal line beneath the standard line. Since the standard and comparison intervals are equated on the basis of clock time, the length of the comparison line in relation to the standard line provides a *direct* measure of the relative duration of the two intervals in terms of the subject's *experience*. Figure 20 illustrates the following example: a standard interval of 10 seconds is presented under white light, and a line 10 cm in length is drawn to represent it. A comparison interval of 10 seconds is presented under coloured light, and the subject draws a line to indicate the subjective duration of this interval, making the line, say, 12 cm in length.

Since the comparison line is longer than the standard, it is clear that the comparison interval appeared to the subject to have a longer duration than the standard, the exact relative duration being in the ratio of 12:10.

This technique provides an estimate of time experience

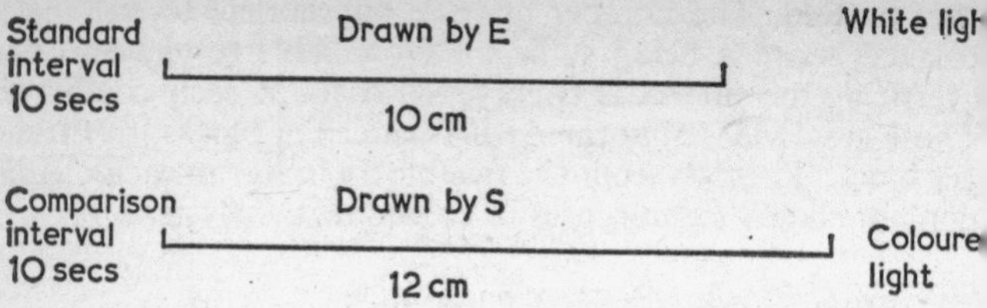

| Standard interval 10 secs | Drawn by E | White ligh |
| | 10 cm | |

| Comparison interval 10 secs | Drawn by S | Coloure light |
| | 12 cm | |

Fig. 20 *Visual representation of subjective duration of standar and comparison intervals*

under coloured light in relation to that under white light. The experimental hypothesis, however, demands a comparison between time experience under red and blue light. This demand may be met by matching clock durations of presentation intervals across the experimental conditions for each subject, a particular interval used in one condition being paired with an interval in the other condition. Thus, each Red and Blue pair of subjective estimates of duration will be based on identical standards, and a direct comparison between them and therefore between the two conditions, is possible. This argument is exemplified diagrammatically in Fig. 21.

(Although a technique by which direct comparisons between red and blue intervals made by the subject could be employed in this experiment, it would be associated with certain problems. For example, it would fall victim to the 'time-order' error affecting time judgements, in which the second of two equal intervals is perceived as the longer, and which would necessitate further counterbalancing measures. The technique described in the preceding paragraphs was devised to avoid such complications. For although it does not avoid possible 'time-order' error effects between white and coloured intervals, these are irrelevant to the final analysis of a red-blue comparison, and, assuming that the effect of being preceded by white light is the same for both red and blue intervals, the coloured intervals are equated by virtue of always being the interval presented second in a trial.)

(iv) *Duration of standard and comparison intervals*

The clock durations of these intervals is really a matter of the individual experimenter's decision. However, intervals of approximately 10–30 seconds are quite practicable, bearing

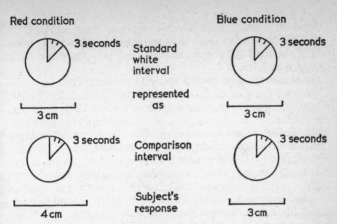

Fig. 21 *Example of paired presentation intervals and subjective experience of duration*

in mind the time limits often imposed on laboratory experiments. If presentation intervals are in the range given above, then inter-trial intervals of about one minute should be used, allowing the subject to relax and recover from the effects of the lights. The duration of presentation intervals must vary randomly from trial to trial to prevent the development of stereotyped responses; the durations, paired across A and B conditions, should be decided for each subject before the start of the experiment. Table 16 illustrates the sort of preparation required:

Table 16 Clock duration in seconds of presentation intervals, randomized across trials per subject

	A_1		B_1		B_2		A_2	
	T_1	12	T_6	9	T_{11}	9	T_{16}	10
	T_2	17	T_7	11	T_{12}	10	T_{17}	14
S_1:	T_3	8	T_8	8	T_{13}	18	T_{18}	9
	T_4	11	T_9	17	T_{14}	10	T_{19}	10
	T_5	9	T_{10}	12	T_{15}	14	T_{20}	18

T = trial

In this table A_1 and B_1, and B_2 and A_2 intervals are paired, though the *order* is not repeated.

117

(v) *Apparatus*

    (*a*) A stop watch, with which to measure time intervals.

    (*b*) Large sheets of plain or lined (but not squared) paper on which standard lines are prepared and subjects draw their comparison lines.

    (*c*) Materials to produce a coloured environment.

You can use goggles with interchangeable red, blue or plain lenses, or electric light bulbs of those colours. The optimum place to conduct this experiment would be a windowless, white-walled, sound-proofed cubicle; this would achieve constant intensity of light used (which is not always possible with daylight as a background), optimum clarity of colour, and maximum freedom from distraction. If you have no access to such a cubicle a mini-cubicle can be constructed from a wooden box painted white inside, into which the subject can insert his head. Failing this, make sure that the subject can look at a large, white unpatterned expanse, such as a plain wall or a sheet of paper, during the trials.

(vi) *Procedure*

Since this experiment is a little complicated procedurally, it needs a maximum of preparation before starting. Prepare a table of ABBA patterns for the whole experiment, determining on a random basis which condition (red or blue) is to be A, and which B, for each subject. Prepare a table of randomized clock durations of presentation intervals for each subject, and, in conjunction with this, response sheets with lines of appropriate length representing the standard intervals (one sheet per trial is required). Before testing each subject, make sure that he is not colour blind for red-blue colours.

Theoretically, it would be best to disguise from the subject the fact that the experience of time is being tested, but this 'deception' would be impossible to maintain with repeated trials. But discourage your subject from counting in any form in order to increase his 'accuracy' of performance, by emphasizing that you are not interested in accuracy, but in individual reactions to colour and in subjective feelings of duration, and there are no 'correct' responses. Remember to remove any wrist watches or other visible clocks in case your instructions are not completely obeyed.

The method of presentation of standard and comparison intervals has not yet been discussed; probably the simplest way is to indicate the beginning and end of the interval by a prearranged signal, e.g. the tap of a pencil on the table. Thus the sequence of a single trial will be as follows: the white light is switched on (or the subject puts on transparent goggles) for a certain *adaptation* period, during which the subject's visual system becomes accustomed to the light. The standard interval is then presented, timed as accurately as possible on the stop watch, the beginning and end being indicated by taps. The subject simply sits quietly through this interval. The white light is switched off, and the light of the appropriate colour is switched on. After the adaptation period the comparison interval is presented. The coloured light is extinguished, and the subject is asked to indicate (under daylight or neutral artificial light) the apparent duration of the comparison interval by drawing a line beneath the one representing the standard. At the end of the inter-trial interval, the subject is asked to prepare for the next trial. Twenty such test trials are required per subject and no particular break between A and B trials should be made apparent to the subject, apart from the obvious change in colour.

The test trials should be preceded by a few practice trials which do not contribute to the subject's score. A pilot run would also be useful, in which one or two subjects are tested outside the experiment proper, to give the experimenter practice in the procedure.

The minimum total number of subjects is six. Fewer than this would provide little chance of obtaining significant results.

The overall design of the experiment is shown in Table 17, parts (*a*) and (*b*).

8.3 Treatment of results

The dependent variable in this experiment is the subjective experience of duration, and the measure representing this is the length of comparison lines. Each subject will have produced twenty such lines – one on each trial, ten in each experimental condition. Measure the length of each line to the nearest millimetre, and tabulate the scores for each subject, according to the condition under which they were produced, Red or Blue, arriving at a table of your data of the form shown in Table 18.

Find the mean value of the 10 scores in each condition.

Table 17 Overall design of the experiment

Part (a)	A₁		B₁		B₂		A₂	
S₁	5 trials		5 trials		5 trials		5 trials	
S₂	,,	,,	,,	,,	,,	,,	,,	,,
S₃	,,	,,	,,	,,	,,	,,	,,	,,
S₄	,,	,,	,,	,,	,,	,,	,,	,,
S₅	,,	,,	,,	,,	,,	,,	,,	,,
S₆	,,	,,	,,	,,	,,	,,	,,	,,

Part (b)	Red condition		Blue condition	
S₁	10 trials		10 trials	
S₂	,,	,,	,,	,,
S₃	,,	,,	,,	,,
S₄	,,	,,	,,	,,
S₅	,,	,,	,,	,,
S₆	,,	,,	,,	,,

These two mean values are the scores required from each subject for the final analysis. Enter the two values for each subject into a table of data as shown in Table 19.

The difference in the mean values for the Red and Blue conditions (Table 19) will indicate whether the experience of

Table 18 Raw data of one subject – length of comparison lines (in cm)

Red condition		Blue condition	
Trial 1		Trial 1	
2		2	
3		3	
4		4	
5		5	
6		6	
7		7	
8		8	
9		9	
10		10	
	$\overline{X}$		$\overline{X}$

Table 19 Subjective experience of duration under red and blue light

	Red condition	Blue condition
	S_1	S_1
	S_2	S_2
	S_3	S_3
	S_4	S_4
	S_5	S_5
	S_6	S_6
	$\overline{X}$	$\overline{X}$

The score for each subject is the mean length of ten comparison lines, in cm.

time has been affected by the colour of visual stimulation, and if so, in what direction. The greater the value of the mean, the longer the experience of duration in that condition.

An appropriate statistical analysis to test whether there exists a significant difference between the conditions is the Student's *t*-test for *related* groups. (A8, Ch. 5). This is appropriate since the data are drawn from a continuous distribution of scores (lengths of line) and the scores are likely to be normally distributed. (An alternative and simpler analysis is provided by the Wilcoxon test. See A8, Ch. 5.) In both cases the test will be one-tailed.

8.4 Interpretation of results

A significant outcome of the statistical analysis indicates that there is a significant difference between the experience of duration under blue and red visual stimulation. If the mean of the Red condition is greater than the mean of the Blue condition, the experimental data support the hypothesis that time experience is lengthened under red light in comparison with that under blue.

8.5 Discussion points

Before considering theoretical implications of the experimental findings, examine the experimental design and procedure for flaws and criticisms, and for possible uncontrolled variables which could have contributed to the pattern of data obtained.

One immediate potential criticism of the experiment is that the theoretical context and experimental prediction were concerned with colour – that is, *wavelength* of visual stimulation. But another aspect of light, which was uncontrolled in this experiment, is the brightness or intensity. Whether you used goggles with coloured lenses, or coloured electric light bulbs, there were probably differences in the opacity of the bulbs or lenses, resulting in differences in brightness of the two colours.

Since, in the light of the theoretical background of the experiment, it is not only possible but highly plausible that intensity of light would affect the construction of time experience, it may be that the difference in the value of the independent variable (the difference in wavelength of red and blue light) was not the only consistent difference between the experimental conditions; a differential brightness could also have affected the measures of the dependent variable, and contaminated the effects of wavelength. The effect of differential brightness would have been in favour of the hypothesis if the red light were more intense, and against the hypothesis if the blue light were the more intense. If you suspect that differences in intensity of light may have existed, an obvious choice for further research would be a replication of the experiment, controlling brightness and equating it across the experimental conditions.

The effect of intensity of light on time experience forms a subject of potential enquiry in its own right. It could be investigated using an experimental design similar to that of this experiment, with two or more levels of intensity of light as the independent variable.

A point to remember when extrapolating from the results of this experiment is that the findings would be specific to the range of clock intervals used. The effect of colour of visual stimulation on time experience may be different over very long intervals, such as hours and days. The investigation of the effect of wavelength on time perception could be extended to longer intervals, and could well provide some theoretically fruitful results.

If the results fail to provide significant support for the hypothesis, consider if there are any aspects of the design and procedure which could have contributed to this failure. Too short an adaptation period prior to presentation of an interval may be one possible cause; it could be that the time required for visual stimulation to affect EEG rhythms is longer than that allowed by the adaptation period, with the result that the experimental manipulation of colour had no effect on EEG rhythm, and hence on time experience. On the basis of this argument, repetition of the experiment using longer adaptation periods should lead to more positive results.

The general context of this experiment was provided by the idea that time experience is a cognitive construct created out of the occurrence of events, and the specific question underlying the experiment was whether events which do not reach a level of conscious awareness can also affect the construction of time experience. This question was operationalized with EEG patterns being selected as a suitable class of events which were assumed, on the basis of past research, to be manipulable by changes in the colour of visual stimulation. If the experimental outcome is significant, it indicates, in concrete terms, that red and blue light have a differential effect on time experience, red leading to a lengthening of the experience of duration. In terms of the background of the experiment, there are several levels of theoretical implications of such results. The first level of interpretation is that the influence of colour on time experience is indirect, being mediated by its differential effect on EEG rhythm, which implies that the experimental manipulation of colour did lead to changes in EEG patterns. Since different EEG patterns led to a differential time experience, greater desynchronization of EEG rhythm under red light produced a greater number of changing events, and thereby an extension of the experience of duration. The next level of theoretical implication of the results is that events which are below a level of conscious awareness can lead to the construction of conscious experience of time.

Finally, the experiment should engender ideas for further investigation. Some of these have already been mentioned. Another is the study of the effect of different colours on time experience; the choice of red and blue in this experiment was prompted by the theoretical background, but the effect of other colours provides an interesting topic of research in its own right. It may be, for example, that the effect is related to wavelength of light, so that colours falling close together in the spectrum, e.g. green and yellow, do not produce a significant differential effect on time experience.

Part Three
An Overview

Designing an experiment

In the introduction of this book the problem of designing an experiment was described as a decision-making process. Some of the kinds of decisions involved were exemplified and discussed in the descriptions of the individual experiments, and, in general, they appear to fall into three hierarchical categories. That is, the process of designing an experiment may be seen as one involving three 'levels' of decision-making: decisions relating to the conceptualization of the problem area, to the planning of the experimental design, and to the procedural problems. These levels are not discrete and independent – there is a complex interaction between them, and decisions made at one level are often related to and affect or restrict those of other levels. At each level, some decisions are made on an arbitrary basis, while others stand justified; there is no set of rigid rules leading to the final experimental plan. A more detailed outline of these levels of decision-making is given below to provide a structured framework and guide when designing your own original experiments.

Level 1 Conceptualization of the problem
The first step at this level is to specify which aspect of a general topic is to be embodied in the experimental investigation: that is, to define the question to be answered by the experiment. For example, the general topic may be perceptual

motor skills, and the specific question may be about the effect of alcohol on the speed of responding. The question may be formulated as a specific prediction (experimental hypothesis), for example, that alcohol will increase response latency, the prediction being derived from theoretical considerations, empirical research findings, or intuition. Or the problem may be open ended: for example, 'How does alcohol affect speed of responding?', giving rise to a purely exploratory study, without a specific prediction of outcome.

However, even experiments which are overtly exploratory in origin have a *conceptually implied* expectation that there will be some interaction between the two variables, so the distinction between predictive and exploratory studies is minimal at a conceptual level; it operates at the stage of statistical analysis and inference, analysis of predictive experiments being based on one-tailed tests, and that of exploratory ones on two-tailed tests.

Specification of the question to be answered by the experiment also defines the independent variable of the experiment – the factor to be manipulated by the experimenter, and to some extent the dependent variable – the measure of subjects' performance. In the case of the above example, these will be, respectively: volume of alcohol consumed, and a measure of response latency.

The adequacy of the experimental design and procedure adopted to answer the original question will limit both the conclusions that may be drawn from the experimental findings and the possibility of generalizing from the experiment to a wider context.

Level 2 Experimental design

Decisions at this level involve the formulation of a plan for tackling the problem specified at Level 1. This is the *design* of the experiment, a 'blueprint' for the collection of data which will lead to an answer to the original question or prediction. The first decision relates to the number of states or levels of the independent variable to be used, each state giving rise to one experimental condition. If the independent variable can be envisaged as a continuum – which is the case with consumption of alcohol – then it is meaningful to speak of 'levels' of the independent variable. In this case, two, three or more 'levels' can be chosen, including zero level as a meaningful baseline control condition. If the independent variable were something like 'modality of a stimulus', then the choice of the number of states would be limited, for example, to two: visual and auditory.

The next step is to decide on the manner of allocation of subjects to the experimental conditions – that is, on related or independent conditions. A related conditions design, in which each subject is tested in each condition (repeated measures), has the advantage of reducing variance of data due to differences between subjects, but creates certain problems, such as order effects, in which performance under one condition may be affected by and affect preceding and subsequent tests. These problems are avoided by an independent conditions design, in which each subject contributes to the data in only *one* condition.

In some cases, the *nature* of the independent variable is the main determining factor in the choice of design. For example, repeated measures with alcohol consumption could invalidate the whole experiment by introducing uncontrolled cumulative effects of alcohol; here the use of independent conditions is clearly indicated.

The experiments described in this book are based on only one independent variable but it is possible to incorporate several variables within a single design, so that a number of questions about the effects of the variables on a single measure of subjects' performance may be answered simultaneously by one experiment. In the case of the 'response speed' example used earlier, a second query may be, 'Does response speed depend on the limb (hand or foot) with which a response is made?' This would introduce a second independent variable, with two states, giving rise to a six condition design. This is shown in Figure 22 as an independent conditions design, but it is feasible to have a 'mixed' design, independent measures for one variable, related measures for the other (for example, the same subject could be used for hand and foot responses). Information about the way in which the two variables interact will be revealed by this design. For example, alcohol may only affect response speed if the response is made with the foot. Statistical analysis of such designs is fairly complicated and you may not be able to tackle them immediately, but it is important to be aware of the possibility of complex experimental designs.

Decisions relating to the number of subjects to be used in the experiment and the number of trials (observations of performance) per subject should be made at this stage. These must be based on considerations about obtaining reliable data without enormous variance, and the feasibility of conducting the experiment within the available resources of time and subjects.

The final statistical analysis of the data must also be considered. It will be determined to some extent by the choice of experimental design, but will be interrelated with a decision

| V$_2$ Response | V$_1$ | Level of Alcohol Consumption | |
	0	1	2
Hand	S$_1$	S$_5$	S$_9$
	S$_2$	S$_6$	S$_{10}$
Foot	S$_3$	S$_7$	S$_{11}$
	S$_4$	S$_8$	S$_{12}$

Fig. 22 *An experimental design involving two independent variables*

at the next level, about the actual measure of the subject's performance. For example, the choice of a parametric statistical test precludes the classification of a subject's performance into just two categories – for example, 'good' or 'bad'.

Other decisions at this level are concerned with the control of sources of bias, to ensure that the *only systematic* source of variance is the independent variable. Potential sources of bias include: subjects with particular characteristics, which could influence the measure of the dependent variable, and the order of obtaining measures in a related conditions design, where performance in one condition could influence and be influenced by subsequent and preceding conditions. It is usual to attempt to eliminate the effects of bias by randomization or counterbalancing the sources across the experiment, but in some cases, usually where the experiment derives from a specific prediction and the bias would work against the prediction, a deliberate decision may be made to introduce and maintain the bias, often in the interests of simplicity of experimentation (see Experiment 7 for an example of this).

Level 3 Operationalizing the experiment: procedural decisions
The basic design reached at the end of level 2 does not provide sufficient information to actually *conduct* the experiment. To do this, the design must be translated into a concrete specification of *procedural* details: that is, the experiment must be

operationalized. Operationalizing the experiment will involve decisions about the exact values of the independent variable to be used, the nature of the stimulus material to be presented, the task required of the subject and exactly how the performance will be measured, the design of equipment, and so on. Many of the procedural decisions will appear trivial and arbitrary, while others will arise from the specific information required from the experiment. For example, if the information is to be about the effects of mild social drinking on response speed, the specification of levels of the independent variable may be 0, 30 and 60 ml of sherry; while if the subject of enquiry is the way in which the stimulant properties of alcohol change to depressant ones with a small increase in volume, the values of the independent variable may be 0, 1, 2, 4 and 8 ml of 10 per cent strength unflavoured alcohol.

Decisions about the dependent variable involve the specification of the exact method of obtaining a measure of performance; this includes detailed description of the response required from the subject, and of the response measures to be used as experimental data. To some extent these decisions will be influenced by the context in which the experiment originated; for example, simple reaction time may be a convenient measure of response speed, but a complex reaction time situation involving several stimulus alternatives would be more appropriate in the context of studying the effects of drinking and driving (see the theoretical background to Experiment 6). The choice of a task to be undertaken by the subject will also be influenced by expectations about the effect of the independent variable. For example, the expectation that alcohol will only slow down motor movements will lead to the selection of a task in which gross movement may be timed: for example, walking 10 yards along a straight line. The choice of a task must also take into account possible 'floor' and 'ceiling' effects. That is, the task must be of the appropriate level of difficulty to allow a spread of scores due to inter-subject differences and the effect of manipulation of the independent variable. A ceiling effect will occur if the task is such that the maximum score is reached by all subjects (for example, remembering a sequence of only four digits), and will mask potential effects of the independent variable. Similarly, a 'floor' effect will obtain if the task is so difficult that no subject can raise his performance above a minimum level (for example, remembering a long list of foreign words).

Another set of decisions at the procedural level relate to the timing of trials, inter-trial intervals, etc. An important consideration here is to allow sufficient time between trials for any effects of the previous trial to dissipate before commencing the next. Furthermore, when experimental treatment of subjects may require time to take effect (for example, the administration of alcohol or drugs) the timing must be finely adjusted to allow for this delay.

One of the final decisions to be taken at the procedural level concerns instructions to subjects: to what extent should they reveal the underlying nature of the experiment and to what extent should they preserve 'naïvety' of the subject? Some forethought must be given to the actual wording of instructions, since this often influences subjects' approach to, and performance of, the task.

There are many potential decision-points which have been omitted from this discussion, for each experiment generates design problems specific to itself. However, the outlined framework of levels and problems of decisions should be adequate to guide you from the conception of an idea to the execution of the experiment.

For those of you interested to read more about experimental design, we recommend Robert Plutchik's *Foundations of Experimental Research*, published by Harper & Row in 1968. This is a very readable account of the main features of experimental design, and many of the points we were able only to touch upon in passing are developed much more fully by Plutchik.

We also recommend B. J. Underwood's *Experimental Psychology* (second edition), published by Appleton-Century-Crofts in 1966. You may find, however, that you prefer to use Underwood's text for reference rather than for straight reading.

Hints on running experiments

It is always advisable to do a pilot study before launching on the full experiment. In a pilot study, the idea is to test a few subjects who are not included in the experimental sample, so that you can check on the feasibility of your design and procedure. Some of the questions you might bear in mind in doing a pilot study include the following: How does the experiment come over to your subjects? Are your instructions clear?

Can your subjects cope with the experimental task under the conditions you have imposed? How clear are *you* about the procedure for running the experiment? Is any apparatus you are using performing reliably? Are you obtaining 'reasonable' data? In looking at the data you obtain in the pilot study, watch out in particular for floor and ceiling effects.

When you are satisfied that the experiment is viable and that you have mastered the experimental procedure, it is a good idea to prepare a clearly laid out table for recording the data *before* beginning the experiment. Carelessly recorded data can become increasingly incomprehensible with the passage of time. For similar reasons, make sure that you have full notes concerning the design and procedure of the experiment.

An experiment is a social situation, but one which naïve subjects, who have never experienced a psychology experiment, may find slightly alarming. Subjects may need to be reassured on this score. Also, though it may seem too obvious to mention, subjects should always be treated courteously and with respect. So far as is possible, subjects should be fully briefed about the general purpose of the experiment. The extent to which one is justified in deliberately misleading subjects is a difficult ethical issue, but, for the sorts of experiment you are likely to do, misleading the subject should not be necessary. After you have tested each subject, you should describe more specifically the purpose of the experiment and the results you have obtained, or expect to obtain. Remember, too, that the subject's comments on the experimental task can provide you with useful feedback and occasionally some real insight into the processes underlying the behaviour you are observing. Lastly, bear in mind that there is always the risk that your results might be distorted by 'experimenter effects' arising from your expectations with regard to the outcome of the experiment. These expectations can be conveyed to the subject unwittingly by, for example, changes in facial expression or tone of voice. Aim for complete 'neutrality' in your responses to the subject during testing, and whenever possible arrange the testing situation so that the subject is 'screened' from the experimenter. In the absence of a physical screen, quite often the experimenter can arrange the testing situations so that he is sitting behind the subject. However, for reasons of convenience, screening may not always be feasible, so the main point to bear in mind is the experimenter's neutrality of approach.

The point of doing experiments is to advance, or add to, the body of knowledge of the particular discipline, and this will happen only if the results of the experiment are communicated to other researchers in the same field. The usual means of communication is to publish a report of the experiment in a scientific journal. The experimental report is thus an integral part of doing experiments and we suggest that you try to write up at least some of the experiments you carry out. While there is no one 'correct' format for experimental reports, the format we describe below should serve for most purposes.

Title

This should be succinct but fairly specific. 'Illusions', for example, is inadequate, but 'The effect of stimulus orientation on the apparent extent of the Müller-Lyer illusion' is informative and reasonably brief. As this example suggests, titles can often be stated in terms of the independent and dependent variables. Avoid using phrases like 'An experiment on . . .' or 'An experimental investigation of . . .', since all experiments are experiments, or experimental investigations.

Introduction

Experiments may be done for a variety of reasons. They may seek to establish whether or not a particular independent variable has any effect on a particular dependent variable. They may seek to replicate the results of a previous experiment, or to extend those results. They may seek to determine the relationship between two variables. They may seek to obtain evidence in support of a particular theory or to test which of two or more alternative theories is borne out in the data. The introduction section should describe the background to the experiment and should make it quite clear to the reader why the experiment was done. It can start off in broad terms, but a lengthy 'essay' reviewing a major area of research should be avoided. If the experiment is closely related to certain previous studies, these studies should be cited and their relevance to the experiment should be made explicit. If the experiment is more exploratory in nature, then say so and don't try to make it sound more theoretically orientated than it is. Above all, the introduction should develop the rationale behind the experiment, and it should conclude with a specific statement of the aim of the experiment, including the prediction(s) or expected outcome.

Method

The primary aim of this section is to describe the experiment in sufficient detail such that anyone wishing to replicate the experiment can do so on the basis of reading the report. This section is usually divided into several sub-sections.

Design. This outlines the logical structure of the experiment. This includes detailing the variables to be investigated and the type of design. The number of subjects tested should be stated and also how subjects were allocated to groups or conditions. Finally, this section may indicate how relevant nuisance variables were controlled.

Apparatus. Give details of technical apparatus and, if it seems useful, a diagram. If, however, no technical apparatus was used, omit this section. Pencils, paper, rulers, watches and rubber bands are among a variety of everyday materials which do not rank as technical apparatus, and their use can be described in the procedure section.

Procedure. This is a specific account of exactly what happened during the test phase of the experiment. It must include details of how the stimuli were prepared and presented to the subject, and also what response(s) the subject was required to make. The timing of the test phase should also be given – for example, how long subjects were allowed to study a list of words, how long they were allowed for recall, and what time elapsed between the presentation of successive lists. We should also be told what instructions the subjects were given – though avoid theatrical anecdote of the kind, 'And so I said to the subject . . .'.

Results

This section should be a concise summary of the experimental findings. It is not usual to include the full data in this section, nor details of any statistical analysis. Full data and statistical work can be attached in an appendix. Begin by describing, briefly, the outcome of the experiment, giving mean values and, if they show the results more clearly, tables or graphs. Tables or graphs should be labelled and headed in such a way that they can be understood without reference to the text. The convention, in presenting graphs, is that the independent variable is shown on the horizontal axis, and the dependent variable on the vertical axis. In giving the results of any statistical analysis, cite the value of the statistic, its associated degrees of freedom, and its probability level. Also, explain what the statistical result means in terms of the data. That is, it is not enough simply to write, 'This is a significant result.' Rather, for example, write, 'This result indicates that anagrams of uncommon words took significantly longer to solve than did anagrams of common words.'

Discussion

Begin by briefly recapitulating the main outcome of the experiment – for example, 'The present results do not support the hypothesis that stimulus orientation has any effect upon the apparent extent of the Müller-Lyer illusion.' The section should go on to consider the theoretical or practical implications of the results (if any) and relate the findings back to the context of the experiment described in the introduction. You might also consider any shortcomings in the design of the experiment, and ways in which it might be improved. Avoid, however, the temptation to indulge in lengthy funereal lamentations. The discussion should end with a statement of the main conclusions from the experiment – for example, 'In conclusion, it is suggested that the apparent extent of the Müller-Lyer illusion is not affected by stimulus orientation.'

References

In the body of the write-up it is customary to refer to other work thus: 'Gregory (1966) argued that . . .'. In the reference section list, in alphabetical order by author's surname, the work you have cited. For example:

Gregory, R. L. (1966) *Eye and Brain: The Psychology of Seeing*. London: Weidenfeld and Nicolson.

Appendices

It is useful to append the full data, statistical workings, and, in some cases, the stimulus materials. This enables you to preserve all the details relevant to your experiment, and also enables anyone wishing to check your experiment to consult all the information you have utilized. But be sensible about this – the major steps in the statistical analysis, for example, are all that is needed: you need not append a personal history of arithmetical difficulties.

Finally, one point on style. Do not present an experiment as an essay in autobiography. Avoid sentences like, 'I then decided to . . .'. Experiments should be written up from a more detached point of view – for example, 'It was decided . . .'. You may find it useful to have a look at some examples of published reports if you have access to a library which takes any of the major psychology journals.

Suggestions for further experiments

Ideas for experiments have a number of origins. A primary source lies in the findings of existing experiments, either because they are ambiguous and need further experimental clarification, or because they have interesting implications, or simply by association of ideas. In this way, a retrospective analysis of Experiments 1–8 should provoke some ideas for further investigation.

Experiment 1, involving the Müller-Lyer illusion, may be extended to an investigation of the effect of other variables on the extent of the illusion. For instance, the length of inspection period or the role of eye movement may be studied. The experiment also directs attention to other geometric illusions; a study of the effect of particular variables on the extent of different illusions may be a valuable source of information as to whether the illusions are basically similar in nature or whether their underlying causes differ.

Experiment 7, on visual search, is another source of inspiration for further experiments: visual search studies may involve more than one target in a single search, different identities of targets and contexts, different lengths of search. They may be extended to searches through word lists, where the critical features to be processed may well be the *semantic* as opposed to *visual* characteristics of items. Ideas generated by Experiment 8, on the experience of time, seem almost limitless in number. Closely related to the actual experiment is the investigation of different wavelengths (colours) of visual stimulation. Moving further away, the role of stimulus in modalities other than the visual may be investigated. Auditory stimulation provides a particularly wide selection of candidates for the independent variable: changes in intensity, rhythmic variation, harmonic and atonal sounds are but a few examples.

A second source of ideas for experiments may be found in the literature of psychology: a myriad of theories from all areas generate a multitude of hypotheses which are open to experimental investigation. Controversial issues frequently arise and require carefully designed sequences of experiments to evaluate different viewpoints.

Lastly, observations of behaviour in a variety of situations may prompt specific questions and even predictive hypotheses about its origin, which can be answered by experimental exploration.

*   *   *   *   *

Finally, whatever the limitations of this book, we hope that it has aroused your interest in psychological experiments and will encourage you to venture further into the realm of original research.

Appendices

Low frequency	High frequency
FLAKY	SWEET
PRAWN	LAUGH
TASTY	CHAIR
AUDIT	HAPPY
MIXER	UNION
WINCH	POUND
FLOUT	EARLY
ANNUM	YOUNG
REVUE	GUESS

Appendix II: Experiment 4 Approximations to English

Zero order

'hammer neatly unearned ill-treat earldom turkey that valve outpost broaden isolation solemnity lurk far-sighted Britain latitude task pub excessively chafe competence doubtless tether backward query exponent prose resourcefulness intermittently auburn Hawaii inhabit topsail nestle raisin liner communist Canada debauchery engulf appraise mirage loop referendum dowager absolutely towering aqueous lunatic problem.'

Second order

'you come through my appetite is that game since he lives in school is jumping and wanted help call him well and substance

was a piano is a mistake on this is warm glow in and girl went to
write four turtledoves in my book is fine appearance of the . . .'

Fourth order
'the next room to mine silver in Pennsylvania is late in getting
home on time my date was tremendous fun going there ski-ing
this day would end and have no more objections to his speech on
the radio last night played the viola in the orchestra and chorus
performed the . . .'

Text
'. . . the old professor's seventieth birthday was made a great
occasion for public honors and a gathering of his disciples and
former pupils from all over Europe thereafter he lectured
publicly less and less often and for ten years received a few of
his students at his house near the university.'

Appendix III: Experiment 7 Search lists

List 1 Target A in positions T_1 – 100; T_2 – 200; T_3 – 300.

	Contd	*Contd*	*Contd*
CSUO	OSUS	UOSC	CSOU
USCO	CUSO	SUOC	USCO
UCSO	OCUS	COSU	UCSO
SOUC	CUSO	OCUS	SOUC
OUSC	SUAC	SUCO	OUSC
CSOU	CUOS	SCUO	CSOU
SOUC	CUSO	SUCO	SUCO
CSUO	OCUS	OCSU	UCSO
UCOS	COUS	USOC	OSCU
OUCS	OCSU	COUS	SOCU
COSU	CSOU	ACSO	USOC
CSOU	SCOU	USCO	COUS
CUOS	SUOC	OSCU	OUSC
SCOU	UOSC	CUSO	CSOU
SCOU	COUS	SOUC	SOUA
OSCU	SOCU	OSUC	UCOS
COSU	CSUO	COUS	COSU
OCUS	USOC	USOC	CSUO
SUCO	SCOU	SUOC	SCOU
UCSO	CSOU	USCO	OUCS

List 2 Target A in positions $T_1 - 100$; $T_2 - 200$; $T_3 - 300$.

	Contd	*Contd*	*Contd*
OKVC	KOCV	KCVO	COKV
COKV	OKVC	OVCK	VOCK
OVKC	VOKC	COVK	CKOV
KCOV	KCVO	KOVC	OVKC
VOCK	VOCK	KVOC	COKV
CKOV	ACKO	VCKO	OCVK
OCVK	KCOV	OKCV	CKVO
KCVO	VCKO	KOCV	COKV
OVKC	KOCV	CVKO	VOCK
CKOV	OVKC	KCAO	CVOK
KOCV	OCKV	OVCK	OKCV
COKV	CKOV	OKVC	CKVO
OVCK	OKVC	CKOV	VOKC
COVK	VOCK	VCOK	VCOK
VOCK	KCOV	OKCV	OCKV
OKCV	VCOK	CVKO	CVAO
KCVO	CVKO	VCKO	COVK
OKCV	OCKV	OVCK	VCKO
CKOV	COKV	COKV	CKVO
OVKC	VOCK	KOCV	KCOV

138

List 3 Target A in positions T₁ – 100; T₂ – 200; T₃ – 300.

	Contd	Contd	Contd
YVKX	VKXY	YXVK	KVXY
KVXY	XYCK	XKVY	VXYK
KYXV	XKVY	VXKY	KXVY
VXKY	YKVX	YKXV	XKVY
KYVX	XYKV	XYVK	YKVX
VXYK	VXAY	XKVY	XVKY
KYXV	XKVY	KXVY	YXKV
XYKV	YXVK	TKVX	VYXK
YXKV	XYVK	VXYK	KVXY
VKXY	KVXY	YAKX	YXVK
XVKY	VXKY	KXVY	VYXK
KYXV	XKYV	YKXV	YXKV
VYKX	YVKX	XYKV	VXKY
YXVK	KYXV	KVXY	KYXA
KYXV	YKVX	VXKY	VKXY
YVXK	VKYX	YXKV	KXVY
VXKY	YXKV	KXYV	YXVK
YKXV	XKVY	KYXV	YVKX
KXVY	KYXV	YXVK	XYVK
YXKV	YKVX	YKVX	KXYV

References and Name Index

The numbers in italics following each entry refer to page numbers within this book.

Bruner, J. S., and Postman, L. (1949) 'On the perception of incongruity: a paradigm.' *Journal of Personality, 18*, 206–23. *66*

Donders, F. E. (1868) 'Die Schnelligkeit Psychischer Processe.' *Archives Anatomie und Physiologie*, 657–81. Translated in *Acta Psychologica, 30–1*, 412–31, 1969. *90*

Duncker, K. (1939) 'The influence of past experience upon perceptual properties.' *American Journal of Psychology, 52*, 255–65. *66*

Gerard, R. M. (1958) 'Colour and emotional arousal.' *American Psychologist, 13*, 340. *112*

Guyau, M. (1890) *La Genese de l'idee de temps*. Alcan. *110*

Hebb, D. O. (1949) *Organization of Behaviour*. New York: Wiley. *39, 48*

Hoagland, H. (1933) 'The physiological control of judgements of duration: evidence for a chemical clock.' *Journal of General Psychology, 9*, 367–87. *110*

Howes, D. H., and Solomon, R. L. (1951) 'Visual duration threshold as a function of word probability.' *Journal of Experimental Psychology, 41*, 401–10. *66*

Miller, G. A., and Selfridge, J. A. (1950) 'Verbal context and the recall of meaningful material.' *American Journal of Psychology, 63*, 176–85. *53 ff*

Mishkin, M., and Forgays, D. G. (1952) 'Word recognition as a function of retinal locus.' *Quarterly Journal of Experimental Psychology 43*, 43–8. *39 ff, 48*

Neisser, U. (1964) 'Visual search'. *Scientific American, 210* (June), 94–102. *92 ff*

Neisser, U. (1967) *Cognitive Psychology*. New York: Appleton–Century–Crofts. *92 ff*

Ornstein, R. E. (1969) *On the Experience of Time*. Harmondsworth: Penguin Books. *110, 115*

Rosenthal, R. (1963) 'On the social psychology of the psychological experiment: The experimenter's hypothesis as unintended determination of experimental results.' *American Scientist, 51*, 268–83. *63*

Thorndike, E. L., and Lorge, I. (1944) *The Teachers' Wordbook of 30,000 Words*. New York: Columbia University Teachers College, Bureau of Publications. *27*

Tulving, E., and Patkau, J. E. (1962) 'Concurrent effects of contextual constraint and word frequency on immediate recall and learning of verbal material.' *Canadian Journal of Psychology, 16*, 83–95. *61*

Woodrow, H. (1951) 'Time perception.' Chapter in Stevens, S. S. (Ed.) *Handbook of Experimental Psychology*. New York: Wiley. *109*

Subject Index

143